Please Paint Me Caramel

Shakti Bliss

authorHOUSE®

AuthorHouse™ UK
1663 Liberty Drive
Bloomington, IN 47403 USA
www.authorhouse.co.uk
Phone: UK TFN: 0800 0148641 (Toll Free inside the UK)
   UK Local: (02) 0369 56322 (+44 20 3695 6322 from outside the UK)

© 2023 Shakti Bliss. All rights reserved.
© 2023 Front cover artwork by Shakti Bliss

No part of this book may be reproduced, stored in a retrieval system, or transmitted by any means without the written permission of the author.

Published by AuthorHouse 07/04/2023

ISBN: 978-1-6655-9142-3 (sc)
ISBN: 978-1-6655-9143-0 (e)

Print information available on the last page.

Any people depicted in stock imagery provided by Getty Images are models, and such images are being used for illustrative purposes only.
Certain stock imagery © Getty Images.

This book is printed on acid-free paper.

Because of the dynamic nature of the Internet, any web addresses or links contained in this book may have changed since publication and may no longer be valid. The views expressed in this work are solely those of the author and do not necessarily reflect the views of the publisher, and the publisher hereby disclaims any responsibility for them.

NOTE TO MY READERS

Dear reader,

This book is based on true events and people.
 Really!
 Above all, it is a love letter to the people I adore and the island I cherish.
 It is a story about belonging and about longing to belong.
 It is a story about joy and heartache.
 It is my story.

CONTENTS

PROLOGUE viii

PART 1

Chapter 1   It Is All Planned 1
Chapter 2   Is It A Good Time? 3
Chapter 3   Dépéché, Dépéché, Hurry Up 7
Chapter 4   Ready Or Not 9
Chapter 5   What Is This? 11
Chapter 6   Oh Dear! 13

PART 2

Chapter 7   Good Omens And Bad Omens 17
Chapter 8   What's In A Name? 22
Chapter 9   Shakti Offers You Her First Smile 27

PART 3

Chapter 10   Everything Must Match 35
Chapter 11   Princess Francès: Nanny Extraordinaire 39
Chapter 12   Social Status And Hierarchies 44
Chapter 13   Keep Her In Pastel Colours And Out Of The Sun 47
Chapter 14   Gracious Lydie And Queen Victoria 50
Chapter 15   Père Laval 54
Chapter 16   Paradise In Sainte Croix 59

PART 4

Chapter 17   Detox À La Mauricienne 65
Chapter 18   Crossing India In A Day: The Feat Of Lord Rama 70

Chapter 19   Deepavali At La Rue Monsieur....................73
Chapter 20   Goddess Of Beauty: Please Help Me 77
Chapter 21   Quarante Heures in Bel Air 82
Chapter 22   The Saint Sacristi 87
Chapter 23   The Worthless One 94
Chapter 24   My First Almost Marriage Proposal...........101

PART 5

Chapter 25   Grandpère: A Man Of Few Words And
              Much Rum..109
Chapter 26   Family History Comes In Different Forms .116
Chapter 27   Forced Exile 120
Chapter 28   The Dance Of People, Fruits And
              Vegetables...123
Chapter 29   Jean: The Chagos Prince Of Tides...........126

PART 6

Chapter 30   Tifi: Glorious Queen Of Hearts..................133
Chapter 31   The Two Matriarchs...................................136
Chapter 32   In The Name Of Beauty 138
Chapter 33   Saturday Morning Cleaning......................140
Chapter 34   Respect and The Fisherman's Catch........143
Chapter 35   The Grand Tour Of The Illois Community .146

PART 7

Chapter 36   Praised Be The Goddess 153
Chapter 37   Fire Walking At The Kali Temple 159
Chapter 38   Even Hindu Deities Are Fair 164
Chapter 39   Yellow is the colour. Bliss is the way 169
Chapter 40   The Gift Of My Heart................................ 174

EPILOGUE 177

ACKNOWLEDGEMENTS 179

MORE PLEASE PAINT ME 181

WHO IS SHAKTI? 183

OTHER NON-FICTION FROM SHAKTI 185

UPCOMING BOOK: *SUNDARI'S FOOTSTEPS* 186

PROLOGUE

"You gather the idea that Mauritius was made first, and then Heaven; and that Heaven was copied after Mauritius"
(Mark Twain, Following the Equator, 1897)

This is where I was born.

This is where I grew up.

This is where I prayed and pleaded "Please Paint Me Caramel". This is where many rituals of beauty and good fortune were thrust upon me. This is where I basked in tradition and love. This is where I fell into the grips of despair.

That's how…

PART 1

CHAPTER ONE

It Is All Planned

"She was not born that way", Grandma used to tell strangers. She has long stopped doing so. Now she pretends that there is nothing wrong with Mami. No one dares to contradict her.

Like a good wife Mami dutifully fell pregnant almost as soon as she was married. She did not tell anyone that her doctor had strongly advised her against it. She wanted a baby.

As soon as her wedding night was over, she inserted the thermometer into her every day. She no longer risked tampering with her status as a virgin. Her big sister Padma had explained to her that this was a good way of determining if her body was fertile or not. She was ready to conceive. She did not trust nature to do its work; not for her any haphazard occurring. She had a plan. She always had a plan. Padma had already promptly produced a son with the help of a thermometer. A daughter followed a year later with the help of the same thermometer. A son, then a daughter: That was the correct way. She too would have her son. Her beautiful fair son.

The astute daily monitoring of her body temperature, every morning, every early evening, facilitated a prompt fertilisation. Her second biggest dream in life was on course. It was now time to finalise the planning of her son's life, from the day of his expected birth at the end of September. She had thought about the details for years; long before she was married or even had any prospect of being so. Her mother often thought that would never happen. Yet, the old lady kept on praying in the temples, churches and shrines across the island for her youngest daughter. Mami, on the other hand, never gave up hope, no matter what others said about her behind her back or to her face; no matter how they looked at her.

She had practised the colourful embroidery to be on the baby's white *trousseau*, the type of nanny, the kindergarten, the Roman Catholic schooling for the primary cycle, the top secondary school of the island, the university and then the career: doctor or lawyer of course. Roman catholic primary schools were the best. The nuns were well known for being strict and disciplined. Only the top two professions of the community would be fit for her son. She had decided it all.

Daddy, her husband, might have liked a daughter. She did not ask. He did not say.

19th July, she is found in a puddle of blood.

CHAPTER TWO

Is It A Good Time?

Grandma's two thick gold bangles jangle on her right wrist as she pulls the folds of her dark brown saree more tightly across her bosom and flips it over her left shoulder. There are no bright colours for her anymore; not for the past twenty years since she became a widow at thirty-three years old.

Her name is Sundari. It means beauty in Sanskrit, the sacred language of India. But no one calls her by her name except her only living big brother. She is called Madame Chetty by most people or *Aka* by her Tamil connections. *Aka* is a sign of respect and means big sister in Tamil. She is not one for closer friendships. Some people call her *Tantine*; this means aunty in creole, our local language. Her nephews and nieces call her *Ma Tante*, the French polite version. Her family is from Pondicherry, the French part of the Tamil community in India. They are very different from the rest of the Tamils in Mauritius or even the rest of South India. They are very French. Even their food is a bit different. They use red wine in their cooking unlike the rest of the Tamil families.

With a sweep of the back of her hand, she sends the beads of perspiration descending along her cheekbone, flying past her right ear. She smoothens the white bun settling on the nape of her neck. Coconut oil has long banished flyaway strands.

At 5 ft 2, her roundness makes her a little on the plump side. Her gaze darts from the bed where Mami is crouching in pain to the big clock on the wall, then back at Mami. She frowns. The beads of sweat are back.

Ati. Ati month for a first baby to be born. Hmmm! Is this a good time of day at least? She cannot remember. She usually remembers such things. Now, she cannot remember.

A very religious Tamil, and a Hindu, Grandma is obsessed with the good times and bad times stipulated by the Tamil calendar and the priests at the temples. She also has her own version of numerology. Nothing escapes this schedule: no month, no day, no hour. There are good days, like Mondays and Fridays, and bad days like Tuesdays. There are also not so good months like *Ati*. There are also good times of the day and bad times of the day. Day or night is also significant to her.

There are twelve months in the Tamil calendar. All start from around the 15th of the usual months. The new year starts in April. The months are called:

Cittirai, Vaikaci, Ani, Ati, Avani, Purattaci, Aippasi, Karttikai, Markali, Tai, Maci and *Pankuni*. Of all, *Ati* is the least auspicious. There are no weddings or house moves during that month. She also says that it is not a good idea to buy a new car or anything important during that month. Nobody knows why. Nobody questions this. Nobody dares to go against tradition. It is just how it is.

Many things are just how it is in Mauritius. Perhaps this is because it is a cosmopolitan island. Tamils, Hindis, Chinese, Muslims, French and Creoles all live here. Tamils are Hindus from the South of India and Hindis are from the North part of India. There are a few Gujaratis, Telegus and Marathis here too. They are other types of Hindus. The Muslims were from the Northern part of India, before India got divided into two by the British: Pakistan and India. Creoles are the descendants of the slaves, who were brought to work in the sugar cane plantations from East Africa, mainly Zanzibar. All our ancestors came by boat three generations ago. Before that there were only birds. This is because Mauritius is a volcanic island. One day a volcano erupted in the middle of the Indian Ocean and here it was.

Since independence was gained from Great Britain two years ago in 1968, our government has been trying to make sure that every culture is honoured. So, New Year's Day is celebrated several times throughout the year. Tamils like my family enjoy *Varusha Pirrapu* in mid-April. For the Chinese community, the Lunar New Year also called Spring Festival is in either January or February. Telegus celebrate *Ugadi*, their New Year, in March. There is another New Year celebration in October or November for the Gujarati people. Of course, we all celebrate New Year's Day on the first of January too. Everybody uses the Gregorian calendar all the time too.

Biting her bottom lip, Grandma fidgets with her *mundani*, the end of her saree. She is usually the ruling matriarch; an iron hand, no velvet glove. Today, she is troubled; deeply troubled. Like all Tamils, she uses the Tamil calendar to celebrate religious festivals, set weddings and to verify fortunate times. That baby was expected in a good month. It is now *Ati*; too early. Born at the wrong time, a baby can bring great misfortune to a family.

CHAPTER THREE

Dépéché, Dépéché, Hurry Up

Some patches of red start to surface on Grandma's flawless white plump face. One would have thought that having given birth to six children and a stillborn baby; she would have been better equipped to deal with early labour. It is not so.

Bending into the back of the car, Grandma pulls Mami's dress over her knees. Decorum must always be maintained. Slamming the door shut, she strides to the other side to get in next to her. Daddy runs back into the house to collect a small brown suitcase, in which he has thrown some essentials: a night dress, its matching dressing gown, two clean towels and Mami's toothbrush. He packs these neatly in the small suitcase. Mami would never wear crumpled clothes. He grabs the used toothpaste and soap from the bathroom and puts them into a plastic bag. She has a few vanity cases, but he cannot remember where they are kept. He cannot think clearly. He dashes into the kitchen to fetch her porcelain cup and saucer. She hates anything plastic. He will take the rest later.

She will tell him what else she needs. She will tell him what to do.

Mami looks dismayed. For one who plans everything with diligence and precision, going into labour a month and a half early is difficult to comprehend. She looks at her mother for reassurance. Grandma has her eyes closed in prayer. She tries to take deep breaths; manages small gulps. She cups her tight tummy with her hands. The warmth of her hands does not help.

"Dépêchez!", she cries out. "Quickly!"

The car speeds to L'Hôpital Civil, the main hospital of the capital, Port-Louis. Three streets later, they arrive. There are no speed restrictions. Health and safety regulations do not exist here.

A speedy birth is expected. All will be well. The prayers will be answered.

CHAPTER FOUR

Ready Or Not

.. almost 20 hours later
Sunday afternoon became night. Night became day
Monday 20th July 1970

10:00 am: The baby still does not want to budge.

As her doctor had told her many years ago and more recently when she became pregnant, Mami's hips and pelvis are not strong enough to help her push the baby out. They were not strong enough for her to even be pregnant; let alone to go through the whole nine months. She had not told anyone about this. She wanted to be a whole woman.

11:10 am: The umbilical cord is strangling the baby.

11:15 am: An emergency caesarean is going to have be performed. The baby is in danger. Grave danger.

11:35 am: The doctor tries.
>   I refuse to let go.
>   He drags me out.

"Just look. Don't touch her. She is too small" says the nurse as she brings me out briefly to see the expected waiting family. Savitri, Mami's cousin is the only one there. Grandma has gone to get clean clothes for Mami and told Savitri, her niece, to wait here. Daddy is away following Mami's instructions and getting things ready for our triumphant return home.

Smiling, Savitri peeps at the bundle in the nurse's arms. She gasps.

CHAPTER FIVE

What Is This?

02:00 pm: Two and a half hours later, Mami is still asleep. She has still not woken up from the anaesthesia for the caesarean.

"Look Madame. *Guettez*. Look at your baby. Wake up. *Levez*. Wake up Madame. Look at your baby daughter. *Guette ou tifi*", implores the young nurse. She stands limply next to the bed unsure what to do. Dressed in a loose white uniform, she almost blends in with the white partitions surrounding Mami's bed.

"Madame, wake up. Wake up. Look at your baby. Look at your daughter", she pleads nudging Mami's shoulder. "Wake up. Wake up Madame. Look at your daughter". She presses her shoulder harder. She gets no response from Mami.

"Madame, it is time to breastfeed baby", commands the stout matron as she jerks the partition aside. She is used to prompt responses.

"Madame!" she repeats in the same tone, arms crossed over the ample bosom.

Mami does not budge.

Eyes weighted by drugs, Mami finally stares in the crib the young nurse has pushed closer to her. Her gaze lingers on the baby's face for a few seconds. She turns her head away to face the wall and closes her eyes.

"Madame!" repeats the matron sharply raising her voice.

Mami does not flinch. She keeps her eyes tightly shut. She cannot understand what has happened; what went wrong. Although her doctor had not actually confirmed the gender of her baby, she had been sure that she was going to have a son. It had all been so clear in her mind, in her heart.

It is said that some people can tell the gender of a baby from the shape or size of the pregnant woman's tummy. She had met no such person. Yet, she had been certain.

This is not what she had planned. This is not how it is meant to be.

It is all wrong. It looks all wrong.

CHAPTER SIX

Oh Dear!

I am It.

I am no son.

I am a girl.

I have just destroyed the prestige that a first-born son would have instantly granted my parents in our Hindu world. My mother's dignity and status as a wife, as a woman, has just been lowered. I shattered her dream. I am no *premier lot*, first class prize, as sons are referred to in traditional Mauritian terms. I am not the blessing of a son as sought after in our Hindu circles. In both worlds, I am wrong. I am a girl.

I am a girl.

And I am tiny.

Still, there is something else that is much worse about me. There is something else that I would be burdened by for the rest of my life. There is something else that my parents would be plighted by.

It is the colour of my skin.

It is the wrong shade of brown.

I am the wrong shade of brown.
I am the wrong shade of brown skin.
I am dark.
Caramel is beautiful. I am cinnamon.
I am the wrong colour for my Indian family.
I am the wrong colour for my culture
I am the wrong colour for my world.
I am cinnamon. I needed to be caramel.
What will come of me?
How will I cope?
How will I survive?
How will I become caramel?

PART 2

CHAPTER SEVEN

Good Omens And Bad Omens

A few days later, Mami and I come home from the hospital. There is great relief that we are both alive. Mami's health had often caused concern during her pregnancy and the umbilical cord had almost killed me. There is some joy about the birth of a new baby. I have surprised all the doctors with my fast progress. Although premature, I am stronger than any doctor had found normal at the hospital. They expected me to spend a while in the incubator. I defied all their diagnoses. A couple of days and I made the incubator redundant. So Mami was able to bring me home with her when she left the hospital.

With a meticulously written note stating the time and day of my birth neatly folded in her black handbag, Grandma has come to consult the head priest and pray at the *Mariammen* temple. *Mariammen* is the goddess mother.

Today is Thursday. There are not many devotees around. On Tuesdays and Fridays, across the island, temples dedicated to goddesses are very

Shakti Bliss

busy. Mostly women and girls come to pray on those days but there are some men too. These are the days, which are also dedicated to fasting for the goddesses' blessings.

Friday is the most popular and I think the more powerful for fasting. It has to do with *Bhakti*: the strength of your faith and devotion. We are not allowed to eat meat, fish, egg or chicken on fasting days. No animal products are allowed expect for milk. Milk products such as cheese, ghee, butter and yoghurt are also allowed. Yoghurt and ghee are recommended as they have a cooling effect on our temperament. They help us stay serene and peaceful; ideal states for the devotees.

Grandma is praying at the *Mariammen* shrine to ask for blessings for me before her special meeting with the head priest. She is also here to give thanks to the goddess that I was born alive. The solar calendar and book, which the head priest will consult, will indicate not only the auspiciousness of my time of birth but just as importantly, will dictate the first syllable of my spiritual name: the first sound. This is a precise process. No vague reference such as late morning or weekday is acceptable.

She takes a range of items from her rattan basket and puts them on the narrow wooden table. Gracefully, she arranges a dark brown coconut, an apple and three bananas on the *tambaloum*. This circular brass tray she only uses for prayers

Please Paint Me Caramel

at temples. As they catch light, the intricate flower designs carved in the brass sparkle against her busy white hands. She places a flawless beetle-nut leaf next to the fruits. No damaged goods would do for the gods. On it, she installs a white frangipane flower, a pale brown beetle-nut and a stack of small clear camphor squares. She props the flower. Gripping a banana, with a sharp movement she pricks its skin with three sandal sticks. Holding these together with one hand, she strikes a match, lets the tips catch the flame and releases. The sandalwood smokes quickly and strongly. She arranges the end of her saree over her shoulders and firmly around her. Not an inch of bare flesh from her mid rift or from the nape of her neck is on show. Handbag over her left forearm, she proceeds to the shrine.

She tries to hide her annoyance when she notices that it is the younger priest, who is conducting prayers today. Usually, she will only allow top priests to conduct her prayers. This young priest is popular though. People say that he takes his time to do the *archané*, the prayer, diligently and properly even when there is a queue of people waiting. There is not enough time for her to wait for the main priest today. This one will have to do. For a second, she wonders about his wife. Her mother had been very ill.

It is mandatory for Tamil and Hindu priests to be married to be able to conduct ceremonies like weddings and blessings. Like our main male deities, Shiva, Brahma and Vishnu they too must have their female consort. It has to do with balancing the male and the female elements; yin and yang the Hindu way.

The painted statue of the Goddess Mother is dressed elaborately in gold chains, gold and colourful bangles and a bright pink *saree*. She is poised on what looks like a throne at the end of a smaller room. No one is allowed to touch her. She remains pure.

Handing the brass tray over, Grandma kneels on the marble floor and bends forward until her forehead touches the ground. This is a sign of reverence to the goddess. With his machete the young priest strikes open the coconut. One blow, a smooth edge, two almost equal halves: this is a good omen. A small smile of relief escapes from the corner of Grandma's lips.

She wraps the small packet of ash that the priest gives her for me carefully in a clean new white handkerchief. This was made by hand especially for her. She hardly glances at it. The embroidery of white flowers in the corners is delicate and sophisticated. White is the colour of widows and purity in Hinduism. Purity is also associated with yellow or orange. This is why *sanyasis*, Hindu monks, and firewalkers wear yellow or orange outfits.

Verifying that the bundle is secure, she places

Please Paint Me Caramel

it carefully in her handbag. This is a precious. Spillage would be unforgivable. The brass tray, flower and half coconut back in her basket, she makes her way briskly to the head priest's meeting room. Her heart is beating faster. She is nervous about this baby.

There are mixed aspects to my birth time. Day: Monday, is excellent. Time: the specific time of 11:35 in the morning is acceptable. Month: *Ati*, is bad. Many rituals will have to be performed throughout my life to redress the balance of positivity.

CHAPTER EIGHT

What's In A Name?

Grandma, Mami and Daddy sit solemnly in the lounge. Mami and Daddy are close by each other on the rattan armchairs. Grandma sits across on the wider one. They all look tense, very serious. They are choosing my name. For something so intimate, one could have expected them to sit almost huddled in some kind of powwow. It is not so. They are on distinct armchairs.

"Sha. Sha. This is what the sacred book at the temple shows." announces Grandma clearing her throat

For a while they sit in silence, each deep in thought.

Grandma coughs and clears her throat again. This indicates that the proceeding is starting.

"We must consider that she is born during *Ati*", she spits with disdain. She still has not gotten over that child being born in *Ati*.

A few minutes later, she sets the brainstorming session in motion.

Please Paint Me Caramel

"Shanti. Peace. This is a good name. Gentle and benevolent."

She pauses. It appears that she is waiting for Mami and Daddy's views. She frowns.

"No. This would not do. This baby will need more. More strength!"

Shanti is dismissed before Mami and Daddy have had a chance to react to her proposition.

"Something traditional?" she offers a few sighs later.

Silence again.

"Shakuntala?" ventures Mami tentatively

"No! She was left behind by her new husband and had much suffering in love. This girl already has a widow's peak on her hairline. No need to bring any more misfortune on her." chides Grandma.

Even though I am born early, I have a nice head of black hair. Interestingly, something very rare, I display a well pronounced widow's peak on my brow. My hairline looks like a bow above my forehead. This makes my face look like the shape of a heart. Face reading practitioners in the Western world associate this with magnetism but according to Grandma, for Hindus this is linked to widowhood.

"Shakuntala is out of question", she firmly asserts.

Shakuntala is not someone whom they know but a character from Hindu mythology. The story of a character is considered carefully before its name is bestowed on anyone. As a baby, Shakuntala had to be abandoned by her mother. When she finally fell in love and was married, her new husband left her shortly after the wedding to pursue his war duties. Because she had been cursed, he did not recognise her when he came back years later. He did after a while though; that is only when she managed to prove who she was. She suffered a lot in the meantime. Grandma is convinced that bad luck in love is sure to fall upon anyone given that name.

"Sharmilla perhaps?" softly tries Mami again, trying to appease Grandma.

"There is already a Sharmila in the family", grunts the old lady exasperated.

Daddy remains silent. His face is blank but he is frowning; ever so slightly. Is he thinking about names too?

"Sha... Shavriti... Sharma..." Grandma rolls one name after another on her tongue.

"Shamini... Shalini... Shakti... Shakti."

She closes her eyes, takes a deep breath. S-h-a-k-t-i, she says slower, articulating each syllable. She repeats the name over and over.

Mami and Daddy look at her. They peep at each other. They are unsure about what they must do. Are they meant to close their eyes too? Are they meant to say the name too? They have never been to a naming session before. This is usually a very private affair.

"Shakti!", announces Grandma triumphantly. "This is what it must be. Power. The Supreme Goddess. We must do what we can to help her."

Shak in Sanskrit means to be able. Shakti means sacred force or empowerment. In Hinduism, it represents the dynamic forces that are thought to move through the entire universe. Shakti is the personification of divine feminine creative power. Not only is she responsible for creation, she is also the agent of all change. Shakti is cosmic existence as well as liberation. She depends on no-one yet is interdependent with the entire universe. This is a powerful name. This is power.

Mami and Daddy look at each other. Each knows what the other is thinking: "Thank God, she did not come up with something horrid!". Daddy arches his eyebrows at Mami. He grins at her. She smiles back. They agree with their eyes. They like the name.

Mami always liked the name Pearl. As a middle name, she thought it very exotic. But how could anyone call this brown face Pearl? She does not mention the name. She keeps quiet. I guess she had not yet seen a black pearl.

Grandma acknowledges their silence as a sign that she is right. She concludes the proceedings with a single word: "*Bon*. Good."

"The baby will be named Shakti. The baby will be named after The Great Divine Mother" she concludes.

Shakti Bliss

"Om Shakti. Thank you Goddess Mother for this blessing" she whispers as she bows her head in gratitude to the universe. Palms touching in the prayer position, she remains quiet and still for a while.

Mami and Daddy stare at her, still clueless about what to do.

CHAPTER NINE

Shakti Offers You Her First Smile

Grandma, being very traditional, follows the old religion as old customs are referred to. She adheres to the practice of ancient Hinduism. In my country, we have the new ways and the old ways. I make sense of these by calling the former more modern. There are so many customs and rituals that they sometimes appear in both the new ways and the old ways. It always amazes me when people want to adopt Hinduism. It is so complicated.

For eight days after my return home, just like in many fairy tales, only a few very close relatives and friends were allowed near me. Grandma said that this is because babies are very sensitive to people's energies. So, they need to be protected from too much exposure. After eight days, more family members and friends could visit but these were still close ones. It is only after forty days that everyone would be able to visit and see me.

Grandma has conducted a set of rituals and practices with me since the day I came home.

These are performed to awaken my baby's senses so that I may adapt more easily to my new world. Indeed, it is a big difference from my mother's womb to this complex place. She does this to help ease my soul into its new body and environment. Slowly day after day, for forty days she performs many activities and rituals to help awaken my five senses.

Dipping her elbow in the water, Grandma checks the temperature. Too hot, this will create too much *Pitta*, fire in the baby. Too cold, it will create too much *Kapha*, lethargy. The water must be just right. Other people might have thought that hot water could burn the baby and too cold might make the baby catch a chill; Not her.

She unscrews the glass jar containing a bright powder the colour of orange and yellow mixed together. *Saffran vert*: turmeric. She plunges a teaspoon in and scatters some powder over the water. Screwing the jar close, she places it on the shelf behind her. She has a different jar on her shelf of spices in the kitchen. These are kept for cooking or drinking. In Tamil customs and across the island, *Saffran vert* is used to cleanse and purity. This is why it is used to wash children when they have measles and also to protect firewalkers at the temples.

Holding me firmly, over the bucket of water and in the crook of her left bent arm, she uses her fingers to gently pour water over my body. Like

Please Paint Me Caramel

the neck of an elegant white swan, her right hand gracefully dives into the bucket, scoops some water and lets it flow from her palm onto me. Water spills from my body back into the bucket. Each time, she waits until the last drops have fallen onto me before starting this hand and arm dance again. Gently this dance makes its way from the top of my neck to my feet. A handful of water flowing from her palm onto my neck. Another palmful onto my chest. A palmful onto my tummy. Another onto my legs. Onto my feet.

She smiles. This adds to my comfort and ease. I trust her firm arm under my tiny body. The flow of water and the droplets are meant to awaken my sense of touch. She gently glides her fingers slowly from my hairline, over my forehead, down over my eyelids. I close my eyes. I know what is coming next. A big scoop of water lands on top of my head, followed swiftly by a little bit of water on my face. She brushes the water off my face; her fingers like a soft goose down duster.

With her right hand she picks the clean towel and pats me dry. With her free hand, she folds the sides onto me. I look like a folded *chappati* or *burrito* with only my face peeking out. There are no brusque movements from her here; not now. It seems that she has all the time in the world to dedicate to just this.

She carefully anoints my body with a little bit of almond oil. Incense is burned around me to help awaken my sense of smell. She whispers my full spiritual name in my ear to awaken my sense of hearing. She softly chants a mantra as she dresses me. Mami might have liked to learn these rituals and do them for her baby. Grandma just went ahead without asking her for any help or even including her in these. So, she keeps herself out of her mother's way and sits on her bed waiting for the old lady to hand the baby back to her when she is finished and thinks it adequate. Anyway, her mother knows best.

Grandma brightens my eyes with some homemade kohl. She has made this by burning oil in a coconut shell. It looks as if someone has put some thick black eyeliner on my lower eyeline. She makes a black dot in the middle of my forehead. This is to protect and to help awaken my third eye.

Forty days later, I lie on my back looking up at the two faces peering into my cot. We are celebrating my arrival on earth. Some close friends and relatives are invited. They will each be given a little bag of sweets as they leave. Others, the ones who have not been invited to the celebration, will be sent a little bag of sugared almonds and anise seeds. This is called *faire part*: sharing the good news. On each bag there is a message that Mami has copied from thousands of mothers before her: *"Shakti vous offre son premier sourire"*, Shakti offers you her first smile.

Daddy empties the packet of sacred ash

Please Paint Me Caramel

Grandma brought back from the temple earlier this morning into a new small shiny brass pot. As with all brassware in the house, this too has been arduously polished. He crumples the paper wrapping and put the squashed ball in his trouser pocket. Grandma lifts me up gently. Cradling me in the nook of her left arm as she does when she bathes me, she dips the middle finger of her right hand in the pot of sacred ash, which Daddy is still holding. The right hand is used for everything sacred. She presses a big grey dot of sacred ash on the middle of my forehead, exactly on my third eye where she had previously made a black dot.

With both hands she holds me up, my face raised to the sun. "Shakti", she announces to the world in a clear strong voice. She lets the light of the sunshine on me for a minute or two. I close my eyes, probably because of the brightness of the sun. This is considered a good sign of respect by the adults present.

Mami looks on, with the almost perpetual look of surprise on her face these days. She is still disappointed about the boy thing, but she is amazed about having produced a baby, any baby for that matter. She had been secretly anxious about her actual ability to do so.

Like her mother, she believes that a baby's soul chooses its parents. She is perplexed by this little thing. This soul has chosen here. Why?

PART 3

CHAPTER TEN

Everything Must Match

Since my birth, I have remained on the small and skinny side. Other than that, I was not at all unusual except when it came to feeding times. On those occasions, I routinely displayed a professional repertoire of ill-disposition and ailments like Grandma. I just did not like being fed. Or was it that I did not like to eat what they gave me to eat or what they tried to force me to swallow? Or could it be that I was just not hungry?

Nobody in my family appeared to be able to accept this. Mami dragged me from one expensive paediatrician to another. Every doctor diagnosed that there was nothing wrong with me. Daddy tried to force-feed me almost every other day until I eventually wretched it all out. Grandma kept on praying for my salvation.

Mami once explained to me that I was so tiny that no-one quite knew how to pick me up properly for months. Whenever they had to do so, they wrapped me up in a blanket first. It was easier to pick up a bundle than a tiny skinny baby.

Fortunately for me, I was born in the middle of Winter, so I managed to avoid heat suffocation. As it was not much fun holding a bundle, I was left on my own in my cot by my family a lot. A small black and white fluffy toy dog was left in the cot to keep me company.

I was born and raised in a third world country during the days when we were referred to as underdeveloped countries. Nowadays, there is no such thing as underdeveloped countries. We are now called developing countries. I was born long before cots came with health and safety instructions. By current European standards, mine would be considered close to a death trap.

My cot was made of dark brown oak. Every week, as they did to the rest of the wooden furniture in the house, our maids dampened the cot's bars and frame with a deep red unctuous liquid called *Furniglow*. It smelt like honey mixed with freshly cut grass. The maids polished everything until each piece of furniture shone so brightly that you could see your reflection in them. Once a week, usually on Fridays, *Furniglow* reigned over the house. Only the bathrooms and toilets remained *Furniglow*-free. That is because they would have been doused with bleach and disinfected from top to bottom. The kitchen had kept its own smell. Only Grandma and the spirits of the spices knew what had created the latest magic.

Like the waxed wooden floors, the cot shone like

Please Paint Me Caramel

a mirror. Like the floorboards, it was rather plain. Dark brown might not sound appropriate for a baby but the cot had to match the rest of the furniture in Mami's and Daddy's bedroom. Having mismatched furniture was unthinkable in our household. To be in the room next to Mami's side of the bed, my cot had to be of the exact shade and type of wood as the rest of the furniture there. The whole set had been commissioned when Mami and Daddy had been planning to get married. When I was on my way, along came the cot.

It was a simple cot with 2-inch-wide vertical bars and two horizontal bars above and below these. As the upper ledge was within my arm's reach, I quickly learnt to prop myself up with my hands. Round and round along the inside of the cot, I stumbled on. I was just over nine months when Francès first saw me sort of walking by myself in my cot without holding on to anything. No one knew I could walk.

The gaps between the long vertical bars of the cot were so wide, that once Krishna, my cousin, pulled almost half of my body through them. Even though he was only a year older than me and not much taller than the base, he managed to pull me so far that I was dangling with my legs completely out of the cot. I looked as if I was straddling the cot like a horse on its side.

"Seigneur Jesus!" screams Francès as she

runs into the bedroom sending the door banging loudly against the wall.

"Mauvais garçon. Bad boy", she hisses at Krishna pushing him out of the way.

Without a glance to the fallen little boy crying at the foot of the cot, she dextrously tries to dislodge my legs from between the bars of my cot.

Even though he was only almost two and half years old, so a little more than a year older than me, Krishna had managed to pull me through the wide gaps between the bars of the cot.

Francès stops for a moment, straightens her spine as she wipes the sweat off her forehead again. She leans closer to me and continues to free my legs gently little by little, one leg at a time.

"Baby, oh my baby, what has he done to you?"

Pressing me against her slim chest, she rocks and pats on me on the back as she sobs.

"Tout korek, Tout korek mo Shaktilin". Everything is alright, she sobs wetting the top of my head with her tears, "no need to cry my baby. I am here".

Still silent, I nestle closer against her smiling; safe with my ever-reliable rescuer.

"Shakti, *mo bébé*" she murmurs as she rocks me.

Now not in the least perturbed, Krishna looks on.

Nobody knows for sure how he had managed to pull me through and how long I had been dangling out of the cot. The cot stayed.

CHAPTER ELEVEN

Princess Francès: Nanny Extraordinaire

Francès was around 15 years old when I was born. Lydie, her aunt, who had been working at the house since Mami and Daddy got married, told Mami about her niece, who was up to no good. She liked boys more than she liked school, and boys liked her. Lydie and her sister Yvonne, Francès' mum, were worried about the teenager. Upon discussing this with the pregnant Mami and Grandma, Lydie found a most welcoming solution for her sister. Francès would look after the baby. Simply put, she would be my nanny.

She had never actually looked after any baby before me but she had a sister, who was two years younger than her. She also had about a dozen younger cousins. She was used to small children. Lydie said that although Francès was far too pretty for her own good, she had a sweet disposition. Lydie concluded that she would make her great at childcare. So, Francès was deemed fit for purpose. Anyway, Lydie who looked after the house would keep an eye on her. It would work out. Francès would be kept away from boys.

At almost 5 ft 8, Francès was very tall by Mauritian standards. Being thin, she looked more like a long green bean than towering. She smiled often and laughed out loud whenever she wanted to. Sleeveless t-shirts and knee-length bright skirts were her usual attire. In spite of Lydie's and Grandma's disapproval, on special days she wore a pair of fitting dark blue jeans. On rare occasions, she tamed her hair into tight short corncobs. Mostly though, her cropped to the neck hair would just be combed back and kept in place with a plastic Alice Band; different colours depending on the colour of her t-shirt. To me, she looked amazing.

She smelt like a strong flower. She splashed "*Bien-Être*", an *eau de cologne,* on her dress and hair several times a day. I liked when she splashed me too. *Bien-Être* came in different colours: pale yellow, pale blue, pale pink and pale green. My favourite was the same as her favourite: pale yellow. It reminded me of lemons and of the fresh iced *Panakum*, an Indian version of lemonade that Grandma makes with Tamarind pulp, lime, spices and sugar on hot Summer days or on special religious days.

Bien-Être is much cheaper than the perfumes, which Grandma and Mami use. Grandma seemed to have an endless supply of Nina's Ricci's *L'Air du Temps*. I liked the carved white holder of the small bottle and its matching fragrant powder box but I

Please Paint Me Caramel

was not allowed to touch these. Grandma never splashed *L'Air du Temps* on me. Mami also used expensive French perfumes. She had a selection of different ones in beautiful small bottles of various shapes. Her favourite is Chanel No. 5. I liked the way she smelt but she did not use her perfume on me. She did not like anyone to smell like her; not even me. I liked *Bien-Être* even though Grandma said it made me smell cheap.

Francès was of Creole descent. She told me that she had no mixed blood, she was a real *Créole*. She explained that her grandfather had been a chief slave and her grandmother a real beauty. They had been brought from Africa to work in the sugar cane fields owned by the white French people. As no-one in her family had made babies with anyone white, Indian or Chinese, she had the pure blood of the African slaves. This is how I learnt why she and I were different. That is how I first learnt about the history of my island. The dates were a little off, but that of course I would only find out many years later at school.

Mauritian *Creoles* like Francès could trace their origins to the French plantation owners and to the African slaves who were brought to work in the sugar fields. As the white French plantation owners impregnated their female slaves, *Creole* babies started to be born. *Creole* babies were also born from slave men and slave women.

Along with my ancestors, who were Tamils,

other people like the Hindis, Telegus, Marathis and Muslims were brought from India. The different cultures indicate that the people came front different parts of India. The Tamils came from the South-East, the Marathis from a little bit more North, the Hindis higher up and to the left, and the Muslims from the most Northern area. I think the Telegus lived not far from the Tamils. Boats of workers started their journey from different parts of the Indian sub-continent. That is why there are so many different types of Hindus here.

Boats bringing people from China also started from two different regions: Hakka and Canton. But the Chinese are not called different names or have different cultures. Instead, they are part of one big community and are now all referred to as Sino-Mauritians.

The Indians and Chinese came to be indentured labourers, the Africans to be slaves. This is how the journey of my family and that of Francès' family started. This is the reason why our families still hold different status in Mauritian society. However, the story of Mauritius began long before that with a volcano and birds.

With slavery having been abolished in 1835, how could Francès' grandfather have been a chief slave? Perhaps it was her great great grandfather or her great great great grandfather. No matter. To me, she was and will always be some kind of princess.

Please Paint Me Caramel

This must be why she has such perfectly soft skin. Skin that looks like the black coffee that Mami drinks in the morning. I often put my hand in her hand. Hers is deep mocha, mine *Café au Lait*.

CHAPTER TWELVE

Social Status And Hierarchies

My island was created by a volcano. For a very long time, only birds lived here. At the beginning of the 10th century, Arab traders found out about its existence but they did not stop over. Portuguese naval explorers stumbled upon the island in the wake of Vasco de Gama's voyage around the Cape of Good Hope in 1498. Our history books say they did little more than leave monkeys and rats behind.

The Dutch Vice Admiral Wybrandt van Warwyck arrived in 1598. He claimed and named the island after his ruler, Maurice, Prince of Orange and Count of Nassau. However, they only stopped forty years later. Even then, it was only because they were looking for supplies such as water on their way to Java. Java was considered much more worthy because of its spices.

By the time they left in 1710, the Dutch had eaten all the Dodos on the island. The Dodo was a flightless bird, which was only found in Mauritius. So, as they ate the Dodo population of Mauritius,

Please Paint Me Caramel

the Dutch ate the entire Dodo population of the world. This is how the Dodo became extinct.

Five years later the French came along. Promptly, the French captain Guillaume Dufresne d'Arsal renamed the island: Île de France. My island was now French. It became a trading base for the French East India Company. In 1721, African slaves including the ancestors of Francès were brought to Mauritius from the island of Zanzibar and the East Coast of Africa. Slaves worked in the sugar cane fields managed by the French plantation owners. Within fifteen years the first sugar mill was built, along with a road network and hospital. This is how our main industry, sugar, started. Real life began. Mauritius became alive.

My island stayed French for a century. In 1810s, the British turned up. After an initial defeat at the Battle of Vieux Grand Port, the British troops landed at Cap Malheureux on the northern coast and took the island. The 1814 Treaty of Paris saw Île de France, Rodrigues and the Seychelles given to Great Britain. These are other islands in the Indian Ocean. The French kept Reunion. Mauritius and Rodrigues remained part of the British Empire until our independence in 1968. Now, Rodrigues belongs to Mauritius.

Even though the island became part of the British Empire, the new British regime allowed the French settlers to stay. The British governor also allowed the French to retain their language and religion. The Napoleonic Code legal system followed by the French people was maintained while sugar plantations continued to prosper under the ownership of the French families. This is how Mauritius ended up having 2 official languages, English and French. This is still the case. Our main polite language is still French though; not English. We learn English at school and the legal system is in English too; so is our parliamentary system.

The *Indo-Mauritians*, like me, are descended from the Indian immigrants, who only came to Mauritius in the 19th century to work as indentured laborers. They were brought in after slavery was abolished in 1835. The ancestors of my *Sino-Mauritian* friends came from China at the same time to also be indentured laborers. This why my family has higher status than Francès' family.

CHAPTER THIRTEEN

Keep Her In Pastel Colours And Out Of The Sun

Francès' job was to look after me. And look after me, she did splendidly. Not only did she make me smell delicious like her, she also under the instructions and with the supplies of Mami turned me into the best dressed doll in my family and of the community. The only thing she did not like was nappy washing.

"Shaktilin, mo Shaktilin, to senti pi!" laughs Francès pretending to faint. You stink!

My nappies were made of soft white cloth. They had to be washed until spotless. Singing Francès hung them outside to dry on the clothes' line. The sun would keep them lovely and white. Disposable nappies did not exist. My family could easily afford to throw away hundreds of dirty cloth nappies. Could it be that nobody in their right mind, no matter how rich, would think of throwing away a dirty nappy? Were we being eco-friendly? Or was it that such things were simply not done?

Apart from that bit, looking after me seemed to

be more of a game than work to her. So enthusiastic was she that I probably was the most played with, frequently bathed and cleanly-dressed baby in Mauritius. A few times a day, she changed my entire outfit and hairdo. She invented an array of hairstyles.

I sometimes started the day proudly displaying an Indian version of *corncobs*. My hair being very straight and fine impeded her from making real ones like her mum did with her coarser nappy hair. Ha! A Tamil girl with *corncobs*! How Grandma pursed her lips.

A little later in the day, we might move on to the *cocotier,* the coconut tree. Francès gathers all my hair in one ponytail on the very top of my head. She fastens it tight with a pink or other coloured elastic hair band. The hair band sometimes matches the colour that I am wearing. I have pale yellow clothes, pale blue clothes, pale pink clothes and pale green clothes. All my clothes are in pastel colours because of the colour of my skin.

I look as if someone has pushed the trunk of a coconut tree into my head. My hair flops over the tight band and look just like the leafy branches on the very top of the coconut tree. She sometimes pulls my hair so tight that my eyes almost look liked my Chinese neighbour, Yin-Ling. She says this is for the correct effect.

Later in the day, we might move on to plaits. Sometimes two: one on each side of my ears;

Please Paint Me Caramel

sometimes high up near my temples like in the children's cartoons on TV, at other times lower down below my ears like Pocahontas. Sometimes there are pig's tails: two, three, or four; sometimes even more. Sometimes the sections of my hair are left loose. Most of the times, they are plaited. It depends on Frances' mood of the moment.

My favourite are multiple plaits because this makes me look like a *creole* baby just like Frances' little cousin. Whenever Grandma sees this, she tuts and rolls her eyes. It makes me like this hair do even more. With the plaits going in distinct directions, my head looks like an octopus. I particularly liked the multi-coloured grips she ties at the end of each thin plait. Giggling, I shake my head and watch the colourful grips dance around my face. On hot days, I am grateful to the refreshing wind on my sweaty skull when I shake my plaits.

When she is home, Mami sometimes looks up from her book and glances at me. She says nothing. When she does my hair, all the grips match and go with the colour of my outfit. Daddy playfully sometimes pulls on my plaits.

With each hairdo of the moment came a different outfit. I was a doll Francès played with. Best of all, when Grandma and Mami were not around, with her I could play outside in the sun. For Francès never seemed to mind or even remember that I was the wrong shade of brown and so had to be kept out of the sun.

CHAPTER FOURTEEN

Gracious Lydie And Queen Victoria

My entire family is Tamil. Grandma says her side is thorough bred. Some of us are devout Christians too. None of us are baptized though. That would not be right. Sometimes I feel more Hindu than Christian. Sometimes I feel more Christian than Hindu. It depends on the occasion.

Today I am going to Lydie's house in *Sainte Croix* to play with her children. That is my favourite place on earth. Lydie, a *Créole* from a good family, had as a teenager looked after Daddy, his brothers and sisters. Many years later, when Daddy got married, to his utter delight she was able to come along and help look after the house.

Unlike Francès, her niece, who looks like a princess, Lydie is the epitome of a responsible mother. Of average height and medium built, she is much stronger than she looks. She too has short hair, but she pulls it all back with lots of black hairgrips. Unlike many *Creole* women, who go out in their curlers under a scarf, Lydie would never

Please Paint Me Caramel

be caught dead outside in her curlers. She wears dresses with flowers on them, in different colours. Hers are of the serious kind. No unnecessary frills, sleeveless or tight trousers for her. She always looks busy; even when she is having her food. She also always looks as if she has something on her mind.

Spending the night at Lydie's place is a rare treat for me. As the chapel of *Père Laval*, the beloved unofficial saint in Mauritius is nearby, she will take me there first; with the blessings of my family of course.

Mami packs a bag containing all the things that I could possibly need. I am only going for one night but with what there is in that bag, I can easily last a few nights and days. Standards must be maintained.

I live in the centre of *Port-Louis,* the capital of the island. My neighbours are Muslims, Hindis, Tamils, Catholics and Chinese. We all have big houses, maids and well-kept gardens. All the children go to well-known top schools. We do not usually play in the street but in each other's yards. The adults are always in well pressed attire and are polite to each other. Our families have mostly lived here for ages. It is *la bourgeoisie elite*.

Although *Sainte Croix* is just beyond the North-Western outskirts of Port-Louis, the area where Lydie lives is very different. The houses are smaller and the streets narrower. There are many more

Shakti Bliss

children around. Also, most of the people are *Créole* like Lydie's family.

From my house, Lydie takes me on the bus; Actually, on two buses. She does not usually take the first bus when she goes back to her home. She says the walking does her good and it helps her save money. With me and my small feet, it will take her too long. So, Mami has given money for the extra trip.

On our way from one bus terminus, *La Gare Port-Louis,* to the other, *La Gare du Nord,* we walk past the statue of Queen Victoria towering in front of the Government House. The queen stands proudly at the beginning of one of the most spectacular avenues of the country while the only harbour of the island tails at the end. Playing my usual game of spotting the crown on her head, I almost fall over backwards. The statue is so big and high that she dominates the place. Although my island became independent many years ago, she towers austerely over us reminding us of the significant role the British Empire played here. It looks as if she is still the real boss.

Mid-afternoon on a weekday is a quieter time at *La Gare du Nord.* The picnickers heading to the best beaches situated in the North of the island are long gone. *Mont Choisy*, *Péreybère*, *Trou-aux-Biches* and *Grand Baie* with their white sandy beaches and warm clear lagoons have long been hot favourites among locals from all over the island. They are known as the best beaches. The steadily increasingly hotels being built along the North-Western and Northern coastline reveal their popularity with international hotel companies and tourists too.

The windows of the bus are all open. There is no fan here. It is sticky. The breeze gushes in and cools us when the bus moves. We are used to hot weather but Mauritians do not like to sit in the sun. As they get on, passengers choose seats, which are in the shade. As soon as a good seat is vacated, someone swiftly attempts to move away from the sun. There are grumbles and almost arguments. But there are never any actual fight, just harsh words and irate people. You have to be the fastest, oldest or sick.

CHAPTER FIFTEEN

Père Laval

Father *Jacques Désiré Laval*, *Père Laval*, was a French Catholic priest, who came to Mauritius around 1841 to be a missionary. The French landowners brought him to evangelize African slaves but he was so good-hearted that he not only tried to teach them about his religion but also looked after the sick and helped young *Créole* children become educated. It is said that he could cure sick people. This is the reason why he has been called the "Apostle of the Black People".

He died in 1864 but he is still very important to Mauritians. In 1979 the Vatican in Rome would finally agree with us and officially make him a Saint. From then onwards, every year on the 9th of September, his glory would be celebrated. I am not sure if this is his birthday, the date on which he died or the date of the beatification.

Although he is not officially a saint yet, like thousands of Mauritians a few times a year my family goes to pray there. So today, it is unquestionable that Lydie would take me to do so.

Please Paint Me Caramel

I pluck two white daisies from the garden to take for *Père Laval*. They are my favourite flowers to give as gifts. Daisies always look so happy. I hold them proudly in my hand. This is like a small pilgrimage for me. I am only four years old so the juice that Lydie gives me during our long bus ride does not count. Only grown-ups are not allowed to drink or eat when they are on pilgrimage or when they go to the temple on special celebrations.

Père Laval lies in a stone room surrounded by a small lawn and colourful flowerbeds overflowing with yellow Marigolds and white Daisies. Two big doors face the road in front of the small stone building. These are kept wide open. A couple of small windows feature on the rest of the three walls. All are open. It is cool here; pleasant and fragrant. This stone walls make it a place with natural air-conditioning.

An old man neatly dressed in pale grey trousers and a crisp white short-sleeved shirt sits inside near one of the doors. Next to him, a small table is laden with souvenirs. Black and white as well as colour photographs of *Père Laval* are laid out in distinct stacks like packs of cards. There is a variety of pendants and statuettes of *Père Laval*. Booklets, stickers and keyrings await the pilgrims. There is hardly a spare centimetre on the table.

Next to the other door, a young woman sells flowers. She too is neatly dressed. Mauritians are always well dressed when we go to churches. The small pink flowers on her cotton shift dress seem to join in with those around her. Varied bunches of flowers simply fastened with a small piece of white string abound on her small rectangular table. By her side, on the floor, there are two big aluminium buckets half-filled with water. Bigger and more elaborate bunches of flowers rest there waiting to be bought. I wonder if she gets some of the flowers from outside.

The statue of *Père Laval* is big. He is dressed in a black cassock and white collar. Although he is lying down, a small black hat sits firmly on his head. He holds a black and silver rosary in his crossed hands. These gently rest on his stomach. He has white painted hair. He looks asleep but he has a soft smile on his rosy face. Underneath the statue, in the stone bed lies his real body.

Because of the iron grille, which surrounds him I cannot get right next to him. Still, I seek my special spot. Many people stand or kneel by his feet. For me, it has to be near his ear. In Hindu culture, you must use your right hand for everything except for the toilet so the right ear is probably better than the left one. I kneel as closely as I can to his right ear.

"Bonjour Père Laval".

I speak French. Not only is he a French priest, but speaking French is more educated and cultured in Mauritius than speaking Creole. French is also used for important stuff. Although children learn

Please Paint Me Caramel

English at school and adults write it at work, nobody speaks it.

There are many people around. I want to make sure that *Père Laval* hears me so I nudge as close as I can in between the iron bars. Although I am on the small side for a four-year old, I am not able to squeeze through them. I do not dare speak too loudly in case someone overhears what I say.

I know that in Christian holy places one should really recite the Hail Mary or Our Blessed Father prayer. I cannot remember all the words. Anyway, it does not matter. I have my own prayer. *Père Laval* would understand.

Clutching my two flowers between my clasped hands, in a hush tone I fervently repeat the same few words over and over. The flowers have lost some petals. It does not matter. He will not be angry with me as Grandma or Mami are when I break something by accident. This is no sacred mantra that has been chanted for thousands of years. I alone know the words.

This is my plea. My prayer to change my destiny. It is very short but I can think of nothing else to say. This is what is most important to me. This is what will make me right. So, I repeat the same words over and over: "Pei*gnez-moi caramel Pere Laval*". "Please paint me caramel *Père Laval*".

One of the flowers has lost a few petals and most of its yellow pollen. I offer the good one to *Père Laval*. I gently place it at the bottom of the iron grille. I strain through the iron bars to touch his ear with the damaged one. The tip just manages to brush him. Having touched *Père Laval*, this flower is now blessed.

I shall keep in my treasure box with my other sacred possessions: a range of dried-up blessed flowers from here, other churches and temples, a small colour photograph and tiny pendant of *Père Laval*, a folded picture of Kali, my favourite Hindu deity, and a small bottle of sacred water from *Lourdes* in France. The little plastic sachet of *vibouti*, ash, which Grandma recently brought back for me from the famous *Pajani Malai* temple in South India, has split. Now all my treasures are dowsed with grey powder and smell like sandalwood. To me, this makes everything even more sacred.

Unlike Mami and Grandma, Lydie does not rush me. Instead, she stands back a little. I know that she is watching me vigilantly. I feel safe.

Lydie wraps my flower neatly in a piece of old newspaper and packs it away in my bag for safekeeping. I hold her hand as we walk away. Today, we do not have time to stop at the Church of the Holy Cross, which stands next to *Père Laval*'s chapel as she has to go home to cook dinner for her family.

CHAPTER SIXTEEN

Paradise In Sainte Croix

Lydie tries to keep pace with me. I keep pulling on her hand.

"*Doucement Shakti*". Slower, she scolds me smilingly. She knows I am hurrying to see her children.

There are seven of them. Four daughters and three sons. Her first child, a daughter, was born on the same date as me. I think she is Lydie's favourite because she is the most intelligent. There are twins: Catherine and Eric. Although being 2 years older than me her youngest child, Magalie, is closest to me in age, Catherine is my favourite. Catherine is four years older than me. Like Francès, her cousin, she is mocha coloured. Magalie's skin is like mine. They both smell like sweets. I adore all Lydie's family; even Tonton Justice, Lydie's husband, despite the fact that he sometimes gets angry with the children for making too much noise. Some I adore a bit more.

Before we go to Lydie's house, there is one more visit for us to make: *Matante* Madeleine,

Tonton Justice's mother. She lives next door to Lydie. *Matante* Madeleine looks like a true *Créole* granny with her short hair that looks like white candy floss. As is tradition in every house, she offers me something to drink. Even though I am not at all thirsty, I politely accept with a bright smile. In Mauritius, you must never ever go to someone house and refuse a drink. That is disrespectful. You must also not rush a visit.

I run ahead of Lydie to find my friends. I know my way.

Lydie's house is my favourite place on earth. When I go for sleepovers at some of my cousins' places, I cry at night and want to go back to my own house. Here, I never cry when it is time to go to sleep. I cry when it is time to leave.

Lydie's house is made of metal. Corrugated iron sheets are used for the walls. The roof is made from aluminium sheets. Mine is mostly of wood. Although there are only three rooms in her house, there is enough space for everything and for everybody. Everything is pretty and clean.

A rectangular dining table and six chairs dominate the front room. There are four rattan settees, *fauteils rotin*, with identical colourful cushions that Lydie sew herself. I like the bright yellow flowers on them. These match the plastic tablecloth and the bouquet of yellow artificial cloth flowers that daintily stand in the middle of the dining table.

Please Paint Me Caramel

The next room is the children's room. There are three beds here, two double-deckers and a very big one. I sleep in one of the small beds with Magalie and Catherine. We giggle until Tonton Justice shouts at us to be quiet and go to sleep. The third room is Tonton Justice and Lydie's bedroom. There is a big bed, matching wooden wardrobe and small dressing table. This is where Lydie keeps the big pot of rose perfumed Talcum Powder, which tomorrow morning she will put on the face of her small children and mine. It does not matter what colour we are; we all end up with white faces.

The kitchen is outside and is also made of metal sheets. It is tiny so the children are not allowed to play inside. The bathroom and toilet are a little distance from the house. There is no hot shower here like at my house. I don't mind.

It starts to rain. There is a small hole in the roof of the children's bedroom. Lydie puts a bucket on the floor underneath to catch the dripping water. We know not to move it. Listening to the noise of the rain on the metal roof, I fall asleep dreaming that Lydie has finally agreed to my pleas for her to adopt me and that I too now live in this paradise in *Sainte Croix*.

PART 4

CHAPTER SEVENTEEN

Detox À La Mauricienne

Long before I had read about the virtues of detox, a thorough cleansing and purifying regime was methodically and regularly inflicted upon me by my beloved Lydie.

Here we are, Lydie and I, under the Tamarind Tree discussing yet again the virtues or not, depending on whose perspective one listens to, of the little white plastic bottle of oil in her hand.

"*Allez Shakti, arrête faire difficile ar moi*" says Lydie in a sickly-sweet tone, trying to coax me into not being difficult.

Difficult! Ha!

"*Mo gagne mal au coeur*" I feigned, pretending to feel nauseous; just like I had seen Grandma do so many times before. Have I managed to convince her this time? Casting a side look in her direction, I try to assess my impact. I dare not get too close.

I am not just pretending to be nauseous. I really feel nauseous. The mere thought of this vile thing makes my stomach go up and down. I only have to think about it. I squish my nose trying to obliterate the smell my mind remembers. My mouth turns itself down in disgust. One thought and this is what it does to me.

"*Mo éna én bonbon pour toi*" offers Lydie, opening her big palm to reveal one of my favourite sweets.

The shiny brown and cream wrapping of the *Bonbon Café*, the coffee sweet, gleams in her hand. I am not allowed to drink coffee as only the grown-ups are allowed to do so. Coffee sweets do not count as coffee to Grandma and Mami. So, I am able to eat them to my heart's content. I once tasted some of Mami's black coffee when no-one was looking and almost spat it all out back in the cup. It tasted horrible. I don't know how or when *Bonbon Café* became my favourite. Coming to think of it, *Bonbon Café* does not taste anything like the coffee that Mami drinks. It is very sweet. It smells like the coffee that Grandma drinks with lots of sugar and a lot of milk. Mami's coffee is black. Grandma's is pale brown. Daddy drinks tea at home. At the big market in *Port-Louis*, he likes to buy a cup of piping hot *Café Coulé*. I watch transfixed as the tea maker swirls the liquid, pouring it high from one cup into another to cool it down. I like watching it; not drinking it.

Not this time! No thank you! I am not going to give in to a mere sweet! I am not going to be duped again.

"Mo vini la" I shout over my shoulder as I dash across the courtyard towards the house.

"Shakti, Shakti!" implores a panting Lydie, trying to catch up with me.

We both avoid Grandma's quarters. The situation is difficult enough as it is.

"Mo vini la" I repeat as I hasten to put more distance between us and get away from her.

Unfortunately for me, Lydie is well versed in my antics. Every month I perform the same drama. Surely, it is not only once a month that I have to swallow that disgustingly vile pungent thing!

"Mo fek boire ça la semaine d'avant" I venture in a lame attempt to fool her into thinking that I had drunk some the week before.

"Menti!" she snarls back annihilating my great idea.

"Non, vrai! Ou pas rapelle!" I insist hoping against hope that I would be able to convince her that she is wrong.

"Allez Shakti" she smiles back, looking at me with those big brown eyes of hers.

How could she always tell when I am trying to lie to her?

"To pou faire moi en rétard; mo éna beaucoup travaille" continues Lydie in an almost imploring tone.

Lydie was so good natured that everyone I know loved her dearly. Still, when it came to emotional blackmail, she was as much of an expert as Mami and Grandma. Today claiming that she had a lot of work to do, she is implying that I am making her late.

"*Pas faire nanien!*" I impertinently retort. It does not matter.

Of course, it does not matter! Lydie never gets into trouble for anything; not even Grandma is ever mean to her. Coming to think of it, I don't think that she has ever done anything wrong in her entire life.

"*Allez faire bon ti fi. To en bon zenfant toi mo Shakti!*"

Coaxing and guilt failing, Lydie is shifting tactics to flattery about me being a good little girl.

This time I am going to stand my ground. I have seen and heard it all before. I too can be good at this game!

"*Demain mo boire li*" I cleverly offer as a truce.

Why not? Of course, I could drink it tomorrow.

"*Demain mo pas là!*" responds Lydie flatly.

Would she really be off tomorrow? Is it Saturday today? She was always off on Sundays. Like a good catholic, she goes to mass every Sunday morning. I am in the middle of my Summer school holidays so I am a little mixed up with the days. When there is school, it is easier for me to remember which day it is. Which day is it today?

"*To conné de l'huile là faire vine zoli ça*" whispers Lydie bending towards me as if to share a secret.

"*Hein?*"

This of course I have never heard before.

This oil makes people beautiful? This disgusting thing! How could this revolting stuff make anyone beautiful?

"*Oui. To pas conné? Li nétoye to endans ek faire toi vine zoli!*" explains Lydie further.

This cleans my inside? Well, I know it does something to my inside. But can it make me beautiful? Really? Is this even possible?

My short pause for thought does not escape Lydie. She pounces on her prey.

"*Aie*" I scream as Lydie's grip closes on one of my thin arms. I try to wriggle out of her grip.

On the small side for my six years old, I am no match for her. I am stuck. There is no escape. Beauty is about to be thrust upon me.

"*Ouvert la bouche*" she commands lodging my body in a firm hold under her arm.

In another swift movement, she pins both my arms by my side, presses the sides of my face closer to open my mouth, unscrews the lid of the bottle, pours the viscous liquid down my throat, tears the wrapping off the sweet and shoves the *Bonbon Café* in my mouth.

Beauty is poured down my throat as my body shudders from waves of nausea.

Caramel world, here I come!

CHAPTER EIGHTEEN

Crossing India In A Day: The Feat Of Lord Rama

As in all Hindu households, the festival of light is celebrated in my family with great gusto. It is celebrated to honour and to ask for the blessings of Lutchmee, the goddess of beauty and good fortune. I think it may be called the festival of light because this female deity is also the goddess of light. What confuses me even more is that it is also celebrated for the return of Lord Rama back to his home from exile.

Grandma sometimes tell us stories from the Ramayana. This is a sacred book for Hindus. I have not personally read this book or even seen one yet but Grandma has. Lord Rama had to leave for the forest with his wife Sita. His brother Lutchuman followed him out of loyalty. After seven years of exile, they returned home. The Ramayana is the epic compilation of stories about their journey.

Grandma is the best storyteller I know. I am always amazed about how she remembers all the stories though. She does not actually read from

Please Paint Me Caramel

any book when she is telling us a story. Her mother told stories to her when she was a little girl and now, she tells them to my cousins and me: her grandchildren. It is not written anywhere for her. She just remembers them in her head. If I ask her to tell me a story, she always says that she is busy. So now, I ask Nadaraj, my elder cousin, her favourite grandson to request stories. She always says yes to him. Then, all I have to do is to sit quietly nearby and enjoy their mystery.

Hindu mythology seems to just like a big Indian family like mine. Everybody seems to be related to everybody else through marriage or by being distant relatives. Lutchmee is the consort of Lord Vishnu. Most of the male deities have a female counterpart. It has to do with the balance of the masculine and feminine energy. Lord Rama is part of the lineage of Vishnu. It all has to do with reincarnation and God coming back to earth to help humanity. Vishnu took birth as Rama to help human beings.

In my family, we do not celebrate the return of Lord Rama but the bountifulness of the beautiful Lutchmee. Being the goddess bestower of beauty, she is always portrayed as fair with pink cheeks. Grandma told me that Lord Rama returned to India. So, as we live in Mauritius, may be his return does not have much to do with us after all.

Something else that is very interesting but a little complicated about this festival is that your sub-culture of Hinduism is going to determine when you celebrate Deepavali and also how you call it. The Tamils, like my family, celebrate at dawn and in the morning. We call it Deepavali. The Hindis celebrate during the day and in early afternoon. They call it Divali. The Marathis and Gujaratis do so during the late afternoon and evening. They call it Diwali.

This timing is because Lord Rama travelled from Lanka, now Sri Lanka, to Tamil Nadu, the land of the Tamils, in South-East India first. Then he made his way up North across the various religious regions of India. Hindis are dominant in central India. Marathis higher North and Gujaratis higher still in Northern India. His chariot must have travelled really fast to cover the whole of India in one day! Tomorrow morning, my family and I shall celebrate while my neighbours, who are Hindis, will do so in the afternoon. As I explained before, we call the event by different names. But as we are all Hindus, all of us shall celebrate.

CHAPTER NINETEEN

Deepavali At La·Rue Monsieur

Deepavali is one of Grandma's favourite celebrations. For three days before the special day, she frantically and continuously seems to be making Indian delights. She neither ever writes anything down, nor reads any recipe. She uses her fingers, her hands and a cup for measuring. It is always the same porcelain teacup. She mutters a lot to herself while adding up. She also never ever tastes anything as when food is prepared to be offered to God, it should not be tasted. This is yet another rule of hers. We are also not allowed to eat any of the delights before the special day. How it all tastes so delicious will always remain a mystery to me!

Dozens of *julab jamuns*, *rasgoullas*, *barfis*, *halwas*, *laddhus* and *nankatais* are all neatly piled up while bowls of savoury *sev* and sweet *burndis* are diligently stacked. Different flavours, different colours, different shapes ... yet they all appear to come together like a magical edible tapestry. But of course, as Grandma is in charge, it is a diligently organised operation. No one is allowed to hover in her kitchen.

Once the Indian delights are cooled down, each speciality is neatly stacked in multi-coloured big plastic containers reserved especially for this purpose. Grandma has a theory about plastic containers retaining smells so these have been bought and over the years kept only to store specific Indian sweetmeats. Nothing is labelled. There are no notes kept. She remembers everything in her head.

Nankatai, my favourite, is made from roasted semolina, sugar and ghee. The little mounds have been baked slowly at low heat. They are slightly crunchy on the outside and softer inside. They are so delicate that they melt on your tongue. Grandma carefully lifts each one from the cooling oven trays and places it into the dedicated big rectangular containers. She separates the cardamon flavoured ones from the plain ones. I sit at the edge of the table discreetly inhaling the waves of cardamon, weary of Grandma's sharp tongue if she catches me. You must not smell God's food.

Julab jamuns, little cylinders of condensed milk, self-rising flour and milk are rolled by hand until each is exactly 3 centimetres long. These are deep fried quickly, then dropped into a big bowl of golden syrup and promptly retrieved to be drip drain.

Rasgoolas, white balls of a sweetened whey preparation, are browned slightly in hot sunflower

Please Paint Me Caramel

oil before being left to soak in a clear light syrup. Trays of multi-coloured *barfis* made with a base of full cream milk powder and condensed milk are neatly cut in perfect individual rectangles and then stacked. The green ones are packed with thick almond slivers. The pink ones are loaded with desiccated coconut. The cream ones, otherwise known as the plain ones, have an extra dose of saffron.

Carrot *halwas* are made by cooking grated carrot, with cardamon and condensed milk until almost dry. This is then packed on special rectangular trays and set aside in the breeze outside to cool down. A thin new muslin cloth is placed over the trays to shelter them from flying insects and greedy ants. Once set, they are cut into little diagonal shapes.

Burndis are tiny bright orange yellow sweet dumplings which have been deep fried then left to soak in hot syrup. They remind me of big rain drops. Grandma dips her hand in the bucket of raisins and cold *burndis*. She rolls an amount in her hand and turns this into a ball. Each small handful makes a perfect ball. Like every other delight, these are all matching in size. It looks as if all the sweet cakes have been put in their own special mould. Every single piece looks identical to its kin. I think that Grandma's hand must be some kind of special multi-mould.

The various aromas join in some kind of trance

dance. Cardamon, cinnamon, saffron, pistachio, roasted almond; all tumble together to entice my nostrils and taste buds. I am very tempted to reach out and quickly sneak one into my mouth. I dare not. No one is allowed to eat any before the special Deepavali prayer. This is another one of the mandatory rules.

It always makes me laugh, silently of course and in my head, that when asked about her preparation for Deepavali, Grandma always dismissively says "*en ti moment!*"; implying that it only took her a little while to prepare it all. Dear Lord, she is such a liar. She has been cooking almost non-stop day and night for three days. She does not prepare anything earlier as she wants everything to be fresh and she refuses to keep anything in the fridge. This is yet another one of her theories. She insists that the fridge and the cold air will alter the taste of the delicate cakes. She may have a point though! Hence, this is a time of the year when her cheeks seem to be perpetually flushed and pink from the heat of the kitchen, from the activity and of course from the excitement. Indeed, I don't think that I have ever seen her looking so happy.

CHAPTER TWENTY

Goddess Of Beauty: Please Help Me

In contrast to this hive of activity of the past three days and nights, the morning of Deepavali takes on a deeply spiritual and reverent tone. Everybody is now involved.

At the crack of dawn, at about five am, Mami wakes me up. Of course, her day started long before. I have often wondered if Grandma sleeps the night before Deepavali.

After bathing and washing my hair, I get on my hands and knees and clean the floor. With a wet cloth, I wipe the room and area where the prayers are to be done. Over the past few days, everyone working at the house and the rest of the family have helped to clean the house from floor to ceiling. All the cupboards have been emptied and cleaned. Everything that could be dusted, wiped, washed, cleaned or polished have gone through our smart hands.

This morning, it is my turn to clean that room all over again with a wet new towel. I do so in my new dress. Everything I wear today is new so I have to be very careful not to let the water splash on me. I am always in charge of cleaning on that day. I think it is because I need more blessings than Mami, Grandma or Daddy. It all has to do with my karma and my past lives, I think. As Maha Lutchmee is also the goddess of beauty, I don't complain. Instead, I try hard to remember to do everything right. I know how much I need her blessings!

Before dawn, Grandma makes the last three cakes. Two savoury cakes are prepared. *Gateaux piments*, my favourite, is a deep-fried ball of crushed yellow split peas, onion, fennel seeds and *carrie poulé* leaves. *Bhaja*, deep fried dumplings, are made from a base of ground gram flour. *Torppum*, a slightly fried white ball of self-rising flour with a sticky sweet filling of cooked and smashed urad beans with grated coconut, is Grandma's *piece de resistance*. She is known in our community for making the best *Torppum*. I have heard so many people rave about these. I feel so proud that she is my grandmother. Yes, I want to say to them: "She is my Grandma!". Many have even told me that every year they eagerly wait for my arrival on Deepavali day. I somehow think though that they do not actually wait for me but rather for Grandma's Indian cakes.

Once the last bit of cooking is done, Mami takes over. Grandma finally sits down next to the table loaded with Indian sweets and cakes. She almost smiles benevolently. But of course, this is not a mere

Please Paint Me Caramel

benevolent festival for my family. And Grandma does not smile haphazardly. This is a perfectly synchronised operation. Everybody has a specific role to play. Grandma is of course very much in charge.

Daddy helps set up the area for prayers. He lights the *cuttuvelku*, the big intricate brass lamp. Earlier he filled the slots with oil poured from a newly opened bottle. He strikes a match and set fire to the end of each of the pieces of cotton wick. As she is a widow, Grandma is not allowed to do so. He then lights a square piece of camphor and sets it on top of the chunks of *sambrani*. The pieces of frankincense soon start to smoke. Everything has to be perfectly aligned in the right spot and angle. Incense sticks and camphor are then lit to welcome the goddess Maha Lutchmee to our home and lives. After all, four of us have offered our prayers, and each added a piece of *sambrani* to the burning fragrant stack, Daddy takes the *sambrani* and the lit camphor to all the rooms and corners of the gardens surrounding our house. This is so that the goddess may be welcomed throughout the house and the rest of our home.

While Grandma has been cooking for the past three days, Mami has been sorting out the display phase as I refer to it. Porcelain plates, glass plates, paper plates, cellophane sheets, paper napkins, plastic bags and paper bags have all been bought and categorised. Every year, my family makes what seems to be hundreds of offerings on Deepavali morning. Every year there is a strict hierarchy in place. The top tier of our closest relatives, friends and neighbours are offered the fine porcelain plates. The next level gets the glass plates. The lower next level of acquaintances gets the paper plates. *Bundhis* and *sev* are put in their own individual plastic bags in each offering. Neither Grandma nor Mami would ever dream of sending a messy plate of sweetmeats. Each delight has its meticulously allocated position on the plate.

I am in charge of the final act of offering from my household while Daddy is in charge of driving me around. We have a lot of fun together as we both thoroughly enjoy chatting to the people on our visits. We work according to the list written and provided by Mami. We must make sure that we give the right type of plate to the right person. Grandma and Mami would never forgive either of us if we gave a paper plate to someone, who is meant to have a porcelain plate. But to Grandma's annoyance, we sometimes come back with bags of delights from other people. To Grandma, this is the height of impoliteness and low class. Not to come to our place to bring us their offerings! What a breach of etiquette! I think that Mami does not really mind as she would not want to stop what she is doing to receive the guests but she does not say anything. Unlike me, she never contradicts Grandma and never answers her back. Even though we know that we would get into trouble with Grandma and Mami when we come back home, Daddy and I

Please Paint Me Caramel

simply do not have the heart to say no when we are offered a bag or plate of cakes. There are no beggars in the streets in our area so we could not even give these to poor people along the way. It never occurred to either of us to throw these away so as to avoid getting into trouble.

The first offering must leave our home at dawn. Just before six in the morning, before the sun is set to rise, I ceremoniously deliver my family's blessings and a plate of Indian delights to our nearest neighbour, Mrs Rambocus. She is well acquainted with this ritual. Even though she is Catholic and so does not celebrate Deepavali, she has woken up earlier than usual so that she is all showered and dressed up by the time I arrive. The offering of the first plate of blessings is a great honour to be bestowed by my family to her. She is well aware of this. My long hair still wet, I eagerly make my way to her front door. It takes me less than two minutes to get there. I do not have to knock. She is waiting for me on her doorstep, dressed as if she is going out somewhere special. Her bright smile makes her look even more put together and prettier than usual.

For the rest of the morning, with a spring in my step, my long black hair floating against my back, I dutifully do my rounds and let the lovely people of Mauritius know that "Grandma and Mami have sent me to offer you these blessings". Smiling graciously, I secretly hope that my own caramel blessings would be on their way soon.

CHAPTER TWENTY-ONE

Quarante Heures in Bel Air

Religion is the passion of Mauritians. As I utter these words, my heart fills with warmth. But the practice of religion in Mauritius, still remains a puzzling enigma whenever I stop to think about it. Thankfully for me, I do not do so often. It is only when I try to explain why until I was about eleven years old, I wanted to be a Catholic nun, whilst being fervently Hindu at the same time, does it dawn upon me that it is in fact quite difficult to explain; let alone understand. Not to me! In fact, I doubt that many other Mauritians would find this confusing.

During the colonisation of the island by the French in the 19th century, as the slaves from the African shores and artisans from China and India were brought in, along came their various religions too. What still appears to amaze visitors to the islands, not me or any locals of course, is the fact that the various religions are intertwined. I don't think that the religions are really all mixed up, at least not in their philosophies and fundamentals

Please Paint Me Caramel

as such, but they certainly are in the lives of the people.

We, Mauritians, of course talk about God, *Bon Dieu*, as we say. Perhaps we see the different religions as the different paths to the same God. I am not sure. Perhaps we have not understood anything at all. I don't know about that either. But the one thing I am sure about is that we never ask about it. I think that it must be forbidden to ask. And we certainly never analyse. Perhaps we just want to keep all our options covered. Maybe it is like betting at the races, when you put some money on more than one horse in the same race. Daddy and his brothers are very keen on racing, so I know a little about bets. Whatever the reason or explanation, all I know is that it feels right.

The atmosphere is electric. It is akin to a fun fair, without the loud music blaring from some loudspeaker somewhere. The hustle and bustle of the people make its own kind of music. The place is buzzing with activity. A few *marchands légumes* have displayed their vegetables and many kinds of *brèdes* and herbs, in various shades of green, in neat piles on folded cloths on the ground. The *marchand glaçon rapé* and the *marchand sorbet* are ready to appease our thirst with their ice-cold offerings. The *marchand gâteaux arouille* and of course a couple of *marchands dhalpuri*, are at our service with their fresh hot fares in case pilgrims get hungry. But then again coming to think of it, one never needs to be hungry to enjoy a pair of *dhalpuris* or some other local snacks. We Mauritians, love our snacks hastily eaten on the side of the street. One can find a *marchand*, someone who sells something, just about anywhere. The place is alive. We are at the Quarante Heures in Bel Air.

Grandma, a devout Hindu, a thoroughbred high-class Tamil as she constantly reminds me, is also a devout Catholic. She has gone all pompous and pious to meet the intensity of the occasion. She is not unique in that regard, perhaps except for the high-class thoroughbred Tamil bit. In fact, Grandma is like many other Mauritians when it comes to religion.

It was not just the Hindus who are a little bit Catholic too. Catholics could be Buddhists too. Most of my Chinese or should I say Sino-Mauritian friends at school, are both Buddhist and Catholic. Some even have a Buddhist and Catholic name. Alternatively, Catholics could be a little bit Hindu or even more specifically, Tamil too. Hadn't I seen Jacques, the grandson of Madame Astruc, carry the cavadee a couple of months ago? Jacques is a real Catholic. Being fifteen years old, he had gone through the system, as he once told me. He had had his First Communion and even had a Confirmation. He had shown me his Confirmation badge. Jacques is so lucky. He could go to the front at mass and have the "*l'austie*", a kind of small round and flat white wafer, which represents

Please Paint Me Caramel

the "body of Christ". Being Tamil, I have not been baptised and gone through the system, so I am not allowed to eat the "body of Christ". It is forbidden.

I cheated once in a church, where no one knew me, and I had gone to the front too. It disappeared on my tongue rather quickly. I was so pleased that I too had received the "body of Christ". However, I felt so awfully guilty afterwards that I never did it again. Still, I hope that Jesus had understood that I really wanted to feel close to him. I never dared tell anyone in case Grandma heard about it. That would have surely killed her! She is always telling me that I am going to kill her.

Jacques had been really sick for a couple of years. Nobody had told me anything about it of course. I had overheard Madame Astruc and Mami talking. Madame Astruc had been employed by Grandma to look after Mami when she was a baby then a girl. Apart from reprimanding me and telling me how worthless I am compared to Mami, she has very little time or regard for me. She mainly spends time chatting with Mami. Nobody quite knows what she does or if she ever does any housework, but that does not seem to matter to Mami. It also does not seem to surprise anyone that she is our maid and I call her Madame Astruc. Only in my house could this be so.

Nobody I knew called their maid Madame. It also certainly did not matter that she was rather nasty to the other women, who used to work at the house. Madame Astruc had told Mami that her thoroughly Catholic family had decided that it would be very good for Jacques to carry the cavadee for *Bon Dieu Madras*, the Tamil God. Mami wholeheartedly approved. This was not at all unusual in Mauritius. I had seen many other Creoles and Catholics do so before, and I had prayed and hoped that my Tamil God would help them too.

CHAPTER TWENTY-TWO

The Saint Sacristi

All this religious ardour did not appear to have hindered Grandma's ability to shout at me. She angrily orders me to hurry up and come join the queue. I dutifully oblige. Standing and patiently waiting in the queue to get close to the altar, my gaze lingers on the various paintings on the stone walls. The queue moves very slowly. Thankfully, there are loads to look at.

Mami woke me up at the crack of dawn, at least that's the way it felt to me. Daddy, Grandma, she and I have travelled a long way to get to this church; even through a couple of sugar cane fields. I am not sure if Daddy had taken a shortcut as there were many other cars following the same route.

On the way here, we stopped at the Sockalingum Meenatchee Ammen Kovil, a splendid Tamil temple, to pray a little. *Kaylasom,* as we call it, is such a beautiful, grandiose and popular temple that it features on most of the tourist brochures and on many postcards. On the way back home, we are going to stop at my favourite temple at Terre Rouge. It is not good to go to two places to pray. It has to be in odd numbers: one, three, five, seven. Seven is far more popular than five; so maybe five does not count either. For us today, it is going to be two temples and one church: a total of three.

In the car, I could not recall this church but Grandma was adamant that I had been there before. Still, no matter how much she insisted, I just could not remember. I was right! Now, standing in the queue, waiting for my time of solace, I really do not think that I have been here before. Why couldn't I ever be right about anything? At least I know that I was right!

How can I explain what *Quarante Heures* means? This event carries such importance to Mauritians. It is probably best for me to start with Lent. Lent is the month when Christians in Mauritius and I think across the world too, are meant to fast and repent for about forty days before Easter. Coming to think about this, I don't believe I know anybody who does that. Well, perhaps the nuns at the Loretto Covent but no normal people; no Catholic I knew.

I learnt about Lent in the *Cathesisme* class at primary school. Being Tamil, I was not meant to be in the class on the Catholic religion but in the Tamil language class with Miss Mimo. But as I was so pious, sometimes I was allowed to skip Miss Mimo's language class and stayed behind

Please Paint Me Caramel

in this one. Soeur Stella, the nun in charge of the class and a living angel in my eyes, pretended not to see me there at the back of the class. It was unspoken but I knew that I was only allowed to do so occasionally. Otherwise, Miss Mimo might complain to my father, whom she knew, and I would have been in trouble for skipping Tamil language class. Not that I minded Miss Mimo. She was so lovely and always wore those beautiful chiffon sarees, which blew around her when it was windy. But *Cathesisme* was so much more interesting, particularly the stories.

During the month of Lent, before Easter every year, the *Saint Sacristi* is exhibited for forty hours in Catholic churches. They follow a schedule. The aim of many Mauritians, including Grandma, is to go pray to as many of the churches where the *Saint Sacristi* is being displayed as possible. She even has her favourite churches for this: *Bel Air, St François d'Assise* and *Père Laval*. These I think, do not include the ones she also goes to because they are easily accessible. The latter do not really count in her eyes.

The *Saint Sacristi* is golden and looks a bit like a dazzling star and light on top of a golden stand that also looks a little like a cross. I have to check what it really means. To me, it signifies the glory of Jesus and the stand is there to hold up high the star and the light of Jesus. But it could in fact be Jesus' cross. All I am sure of is that it is sacred and is only exhibited in this way once a year for forty hours in that said church; hence, the name: *Quarante Heures:* forty hours. I have to find out if every church gets the chance to have this honour. Does each church have its own *Saint Sacristi*? Is there only one that goes round the island from church to church? Do only some churches own them? Do richer churches then lend theirs to the poorer ones, which can't afford to buy their own? I would ask Grandma. I am sure that she would know. She knows a lot about religion and churches.

It is sticky and hot inside the church even in the middle of the aisle. I am thirsty. I wish I was near Grandma. She always has some snack or drink in her handbag. But then again, she probably would have told me that it is forbidden to drink in a sacred place. To Grandma, there were so many things that are forbidden. I cannot remember them all. I wonder how she manages to do so.

My white candle is making my hand get more and more greasy. Someone, I could not remember whom, had told me that it was made from whale's fat. I have never seen a whale up close and did not know if it was true. The candle sure is greasy though.

Grandma said that waiting in the queue was part of testing our faith. The more people at the church meant that the more powerful that church and its associated saint were. Looking around me,

Please Paint Me Caramel

I conclude that this church and the patron saint must be very powerful.

It is hot in here. Every time I breathe in, I feel the hot air come into my nostrils. I try breathing in through my mouth. Would this be any better? It is not. Now, I feel thirsty again. The sound of the murmured prayers adds to the intensity of the place. People are everywhere. Some are queuing like me in the aisle while others are sitting on the various benches and pews. Still others, probably unable to find a seat, stand at the back of the church. Many people are kneeling. All the doors are open. Yet, it is almost suffocating. I notice that there are almost no windows in this church.

Some people are praying silently but fervently. Others are doing so more loudly reciting their predetermined numbers of "Holy Mary" or "Our blessed Father". I strain my eyes to hear them better. I cannot make out what they are saying. I must not eavesdrop. It is forbidden to listen to other people's prayers.

Now and again, I see someone I know. I smile brightly at them. If they are near enough to me, we exchange kisses and whispered greetings. They ask me about my health, then about the health of Mami, Daddy and Grandma and I tell them that they are all in the queue further in front. I have somehow lingered behind for a few seconds too long and had lost my place behind them in the queue. So, I am now a few metres behind. They then smile and move on. It is of course forbidden to talk for too long in churches, especially during *Quarante Heures*.

Finally, I get near the altar where the *Saint Sacristi* is standing in utter splendour. I am taken aback at how beautiful and shiny it is. No wonder it is sacred! Jesus must be there for sure. I am overwhelmed with faith. I hope again. My heart, filled with trepidation and excitement, starts to beat faster. I have seen the *Saint Sacristi* many times before in other churches. But this one seems different. I deftly put my rupee in the charity tin. It is not really my rupee. As I had forgotten to save my pocket money, Mami gave me a rupee shortly before we entered the church. With great reverence, I light my candle from another lit one and gently place it on top of another candle that is about to burn out. I ask *Le Bon Dieu* to please grant the wish of the person who had left that candle and ask Jesus to listen to the prayers, which I am going to tell him in a little while. I am only allowed to stay at the front a few minutes so even though my prayer is rather brief, I decide to save it until I have found a seat.

I know exactly what to say to *Le Bon Dieu* and to Jesus. I have said the same prayer many times before. No "Holy Mary" or "Our Blessed Father" for me. It is always the same words, the same few words, the same plea. I always even add the reason to make sure that God would understand why I am

Please Paint Me Caramel

asking this. As always it goes like this: "Please paint me caramel. Please paint me caramel. Please paint me caramel so that I too can be beautiful." Three times. Always three times. Three times because it brings luck.

What if I cannot find a seat? I can feel the woman to my right pushing me on. I stay put and quickly say my prayer in front of the Saint Sacristy. I stand firm. Three times. Always three times. Three times because it brings luck. Maybe this time …

CHAPTER TWENTY-THREE

The Worthless One

Marriage! Marriage? Hmmm… Where does one start?

Well, marriage in Mauritius, in particular in Indian families, is akin to life itself. In fact, I honestly think that marriage is more important than being alive. No, honestly. I do! Marriage is so pivotal to life in Mauritius that it seems that our whole being and that of our entire society too seem to revolve around it. At any given point in one's life, one seems to either be driven towards a suitable marriage or be driven by a marriage; suitable or not as the case may later turn out to be. To me, a young Tamil girl, this was perhaps even more acute if this is at all possible.

Still, marriage, like my shade of brown, or cinnamon as I secretly used to call myself, was going to be a little different for me.

Grandma had never quite forgiven Mami for marrying Daddy. This of course I would only realise many painful years later. Mami's elder sister had married Daddy's elder brother. However, the latter,

Please Paint Me Caramel

being the eldest son of his family, had from the onset been approvingly regarded as a suitable husband. Daddy who was only the fourth son, was considered a very different case. His parents had nine sons and four daughters in total! It sadly took me many years to understand the dynamics of such matters within Indian families. Now I do. At least, I think I do!

Somehow, growing up in a household dominated by Grandma's matriarch disposition, I was the one who had to bear the wrath of Mami's choice of a husband. Indeed, many years on, Grandma's disappointment still persistently lingered on and even more surprisingly seemed to continue to be directed at me. I indeed had, the bad blood of my father, as she would offer in lieu of an explanation. The only real reason, I have come up with, so far, is that it is much easier to be mean to a child than it is to an adult. I wonder why? I am only seven, so by comparison I am not as important as Mami and Daddy, but still!

Grandma had often used the term *"vaurien"* to refer to me. I did not really understand why she called me worthless; she never called anybody else by that name. Sadly, not even I could pretend that this was something special. Still, what I understood even less is why she sometimes gave me such nice gifts. She would even give me money sometimes; and for no reason at all! Whenever she came back from her travels, she would always bring something

Shakti Bliss

extra special for me. I think she used to miss me; not that she would ever admit it.

Today is not such a happy time. No money. No gift. For some reason, Grandma is angry. Angry with me! Why? I do not know. But that does not really matter. Actually, the reason why she is ever angry with me never really seems to matter much.

She is in full rant about marriage. She is talking very loudly, very angrily and rather fast too. There is no-one else in the room with her. She is in full discussion with herself. This sometimes happens. She seems particularly upset. Her white plump face is red. Droplets of perspiration are falling down the side of her cheeks. She looks like she does on very hot and humid Summer days.

Grandma was rather fat, but in a cute way. She was in fact round, just like a barrel and in Summer she used to get very hot. It could not have been the heat as it was not that hot. We were in June, the middle of Winter! The seasons, Summer and Winter, were not too different in Mauritius except that we always seemed to have water shortages and cyclones in Summer and in Winter, we had a bit of rain and anticyclones, which brought even more rain.

I loved the rain, and always found some excuse to go outside. Hence, I was particularly fond of anticyclones. Anticyclones, unlike cyclones, also did not cause too much destruction; so, I did not feel too guilty about secretly wanting them to come

Please Paint Me Caramel

along. What a pity, schools were not closed during anticyclones as they were after Class 1 during cyclones. There was no cyclone, no anticyclone. In fact, it was a rather normal day. Yet, Grandma was in a very agitated state. Her animated discussion did not abate. Whom is she talking to? Apart from her, I am the only one in her bedroom. Yes, I am sure. There are just the two of us!

Grandma paces up and down, gesticulating aggressively. Arms raised to the heavens. She repeatedly attempts to adjust the top of her saree. It keeps on falling off her shoulders, her abrupt movements destroying the normally perfect and rigid pleats that she has draped across her bosom. In her exasperation to be faster, Grandma's head gets caught in the pleats of her saree. She shakes it off her head. She jerks the saree and pulls it tighter against her chest. At one point, while flicking the material in exasperation from her face, her neck gets caught in the material. Is her saree strangling her? I dare not try to help her. I dare not budge. I manage to suppress a giggle, just in time.

This makes matters worse. Grandma starts speaking in Tamil. Grandma, being very much a snob never curses. She says that profanity is a sure sign of low class. Even though I understand some Tamil, I do not understand what she is saying. She is speaking too fast. She mumbles something. These Tamil words do not sound very nice to me.

In fact, as she spits them out from her mouth, they sound rather horrid.

I sometimes think that Grandma curses in Tamil; not that anyone in our household could tell. As a matter of fact, Grandma was the only one in our family, who could speak Tamil fluently. Mami and Daddy had growth up under the British Empire, as Grandma once explained, and at school they learnt the important languages, English and French. At home, they spoke Creole. So, no-one apart from Grandma understood our supposedly native language, Tamil; let alone speak it. I have started learning Tamil when I started primary school last year so I might understand the language one day! I already know a bit and can speak it a bit too. But it has to be slow for me to understand and I do need time to remember the words.

Suddenly, Grandma stops. It seems to me that it is in mid-sentence. She looks at me. Is it only now that she has noticed me? Is it only now that she has finally noticed that I have been sitting on the side of her bed all along? She looks at me for a long time. It is as if she does not recognise me. Feeling strangely nervous, I smile back at her sheepishly. I do not dare to say a word.

Slowly, the look on her face changes. The red seems to disappear from her face as if someone had made a hole at the back of her head and let the colour drain out. She looks pale, white; even whiter than usual. I do not know why but I feel scared. Is

Please Paint Me Caramel

she unwell? I somehow sense that she is not in the midst of one of her numerous illnesses. Grandma had quite a list of afflictions; most of which she had diagnosed by herself. She was very clever and knew a lot about symptoms and diseases. I have seen some of her symptoms and some of her diseases before. This is not like any of the times I had witnessed her sickness. This is not like that.

Her face changes again. Suddenly, the expression on her face freezes. There is such anger in her eyes. She looks horrible. She looks ugly. My breath catches in my throat. I start to cough. I am scared. I am not sure why. I am really scared. For some obscure reason, I smile at her again. Maybe it is to make her look nice again. Maybe it is to calm her down.

That's when she told me.

Yes, that's when Grandma told me. That's when she told me that nobody would ever want to marry me. Not a *"vaurien"* like me!

Nobody? Ever? Nobody ever?

It feels much worse than when I was stung by a bee. It hurts. It feels as if she has slapped me hard across the face again.

I am so shocked by this revelation that I cannot even answer back. I am stunned into silence. I cannot say a word. Not a word. So much for the viper tongue Grandma says I have. I just stare back at her in horror, shattered in what feels like a thousand pieces by the horrible truth I have just heard about me.

I am not sure how long I stayed on Grandma's bed. I am not sure how long I stayed there. The room is quiet. I don't know where she is or when she left. The sun is no longer making the mirror of her dark antique dressing table sparkle. I am alone. Alone with what I have just found out about me; about my destiny.

The room chokes me. I cannot not breathe. I jump off the bed and run out of her room.

CHAPTER TWENTY-FOUR

My First Almost Marriage Proposal

I don't know how I have ended up sitting on the steps in front of the house. The stone feels cold through my cotton dress. Since I have heard Grandma say that you can get a fever if you sit for too long on a cold floor, I have been avoiding sitting on cold floors. This seems insignificant to me now. I feel the coldness under me. Yet I also feel as if I am burning up inside. I press a few fingers on my forehead to check my temperature. My skin is damp. This is not unusual on a humid day. My forehead is a bit warm, but this is no fever. My chest hurts. There in the middle, it hurts. I place my hand on the area that is hurting. I press harder. When I am upset, I sometimes do this. Today this does not help. Seeking some soothing, I press my palms on the cold stone next to me. I press my hands harder down onto the stone. Suddenly, I remember.

I remember that my destiny can be read from my palms. I swiftly lift my palms off the stone, bring them closer to me. They are white. I wait for the reddish pink of my blood to come back into them. They change colour quickly. Is this a good sign? Is this a good omen?

I look at them. I cannot remember on which side someone's fortune can be foretold. Is it the left palm or the right palm? I look at the left one, then the right one. I scrutinise every line and crevasse hoping that I would be able to spot something. I need to see something. I need to see something that would show me that my fate might change. I cannot remember which line shows one's destiny in marriage. Is it the same palm as for the lifeline? Is it the opposite palm as the one for life? I shift my gaze from one palm to the other then back again. It's hopeless. I just do not know what to look for or even where to look. I start to cry.

Maybe there has been a mistake. Maybe my destiny would change. Maybe my marriage prospects would change. As I attempted to find solace in this thought, I could not help but also remember what I had heard about the lines of the palms. These are traced at birth and they do not change. Hindus believe that one's destiny is decided at birth. This is why the priest at the temple checks the exact time of the birth and the position of the stars at the time. That's why my name Shakti was chosen. A powerful name to help me with my destiny. Do the positions of the stars show on your palms too? On both of them? On one only? Which one? I think it is only one palm. I can't remember which one.

I was born on a Monday: a good day. I was born during the day and at a time that is considered not very good. I am not sure what that meant exactly. I was born in *Ati* month: not good. That's how I manage to remember that *Ati* is a bad month. On top of that, once Grandma had told me that I have a widow's peak so I was therefore going to kill my husband.

The widow's peak is where my hair meets my forehead. My hairline on top of my forehead looks like the top of a heart shape or like a bow. This is called a widow's peak. I personally think that it is rather pretty. The top of a heart shape. That's pretty, isn't it?

That is a bad omen in my culture. I once tried to ask Grandma to explain this to me. All she said is that my husband would die before me. How could my hair show that I was going to kill my husband? That I still just do not understand. At least, then I was going to have a husband. It was still something even though he was going to die. Now I won't have any. Zero husband. Of course, I do not want to kill anyone but I too would have really loved to have the husband bit; a least for a while.

I burst into tears.

I scrutinise my palms again. I tilt my right palm, move it, examine the lines. Perhaps, there was a mistake. Perhaps the priest at the temple made a

Shakti Bliss

mistake. Perhaps even Grandma made a mistake. She is a human being after all. Maybe the sacred book made a mistake. Maybe the palm readers made a mistake.

I sob harder. Tears pour down my cheeks. My shoulders shudder as my distress erupts. I don't know how long I cried like this. Long after the sounds stopped, my tears kept falling. I did not even try to wipe them away from my face.

I am so caught in my sorrow that I do not hear Krishna sneak up behind me. I forgot that he was meant to come visit today. Krishna is my cousin, the youngest son of one of Mami's sisters. He is only one year older than me, but he knows so much. He knows so many things. I think it is because he used to live in England before. He is a mix between Tom Sawyer and Huckleberry Finn, two of my favourite cartoon characters. He is one of my heroes! My other hero is my neighbour Alain. He is three years older than me and is very knowledgeable too. Krishna never ever seems to get into trouble; no matter what he does. It is usually I, who get into trouble with Grandma when we play together and break something. Still, I absolutely love playing with him even though we often fight too. As he is much stronger than me, I have become better and better at scratching him.

"Kifer to pléré?", he asks in his usual abrupt way wondering why I am crying.

"Ki to gagné? Ton gagne batté?", he continues trying to suss out if I have been hit again.

I shake my head from side to side, I cannot speak. I am too upset to answer him.

Krishna looks at me impatiently. He does not like it when I cry. He says it makes me be too much like a girl.

"To vine joué ar moi?" he tries to coax.

How could I go play with him now? No!

"Ki to gagné?", he enquires again in a slightly softer tone.

What is wrong with me? How could I tell him what is wrong with me? How could I tell him my shame? The shame, which I am going to bring to my family.

"Allez! Vine joué ar moi!" imposes Krishna, ordering me to come play with him.

He could be so bossy sometimes.

But how could I go play? He has no idea of my tragedy!

Suddenly, it all spills out of my mouth. The lines on my palms, my time of birth, *Ati* month, being a *vaurien.* Words keep on cascading out of me. They spring out from deep within me. I tell him everything. Everything! Even how nobody is ever going to want to marry me.

As I talk, talk and talk, Krishna lowers himself to sit next to me on the stone step.

"Mais, si personne pas lé toi, mo ava marié ar

toi!" utters Krishna as a matter of fact when I finally stop.

"*Vrai?*" I shyly ask

He nods.

"*Vrai?*" I repeat looking at him. Really? I do not dare to believe what I have just heard.

Really? Did he really say that? Did he really say that if nobody wants me, he will marry me?

Really? He said that?

"*Mais oui!*", replies an exasperated Krishna

"*Allez, vine joué ar moi astère!!*". "Come play with me now!"

Overjoyed and overwhelmed by his generosity, I fling myself at his neck and hug him tightly. I kiss him on the cheek. He pushes me away. Little Indian girls aren't meant to jump onto people, or hug people I think, but I am just so happy. I am beaming. I wipe away the tears stuck to my cheek.

Not even Krishna's *yuk* of revolt as he pushes me off him is going to dampen my joy. Not today!

Someone would have me.

Someone is going to marry me.

Yes, me, the wrong shade of brown! I am going to have a husband too.

P.S.: I never told Krishna that I might kill him

PART 5

CHAPTER TWENTY-FIVE

Grandpère: A Man Of Few Words And Much Rum

Daddy was one of thirteen children: nine boys and four girls. They are all close to each other in age. In fact, I think that the biggest age gap between any two of them is three years. Daddy refers to the order in which they were born as numbers. This is how I remember all my uncles and aunts on his side. Daddy is number five. All of them, apart from one uncle, are married and have children.

I am one of twenty-nine grandchildren that Daddy's father, Grandpère, has. Daddy's mother passed away a couple of years before I was born so I never met her. Grandpère is not the kind of person to have close relationships with his grandchildren, or with his children for that matter.

He liked to drink tea and he liked to drink rum. I think he drank more rum than tea. Sometimes, I would find him asleep at the dining table when Daddy and I went to visit him. Sometimes we found him dozing off in his favourite armchair. My younger uncles, number 11 and number 13, had told me many times that I was not to disturb him when he was asleep. No-one was allowed to disturb him or wake him up; not just me.

Grandpère had a bit of a temper and a very foul mouth when he was drunk. I understood that I was not meant to wake him up. Sometimes though, my cousin and I just could not resist. I thought it fun to see Grandpère annoyed. My other family on Mami's side, was so prim and proper. In brief, I was fascinated by my grandfather.

On the rare occasions that I disturbed him while he was still under the effect of his latest indulgence, he abruptly sat up straight, mumbled some profanity to everybody and to nobody in particular, talked to himself for a short while and then fell asleep again. I kept very still so as not to attract any attention to me. I watched him intently, following his every move with my eyes; not wanting to miss out on any of the drama of the moment. I don't think that he ever knew that I was there and that it was I, who had woken him up.

He was the only grandfather I had. Mami's father passed away when she was eight years old. As I was sometimes left there by Daddy, I learnt to get on with him and we had a sort of relationship. In fact, I shared some special moments with him; that is when he was sober. There was however something that bonded us, him and me. It was vanilla tea and Marmite bread rolls.

I once tried to find out why he drank so much

Please Paint Me Caramel

rum. Instead of explaining anything to me or even replying, he offered to make us both some tea. He did not even ask me if I wanted any or if I wanted anything else to drink. As I loved the way he made tea, I promptly let go of pressing him for an answer and instead eagerly followed him into his outside kitchen. He had two kitchens: one outside in the paved yard and one inside the house. I skipped along as I followed him outside. I was not thirsty at all. I just never tired of watching him make his "*di thé special*", his special tea.

I follow Grandpère through the rooms of his house to the outside kitchen. He walks fast; his body tall and erect. Daddy says that he used to be very handsome when he was a young man. I think him still imposing with his white hair and tall frame. He always looks smart, even when he is wearing his usual khaki Bermuda shorts and a white sleeveless t-shirt. He is just one of those tall and slim people on whom anything would look good.

We go through the indoor kitchen. Part of the courtyard separates the indoor kitchen from the outdoor one. The two kitchens are very different. The indoor one is smaller and nicer looking with matching wooden cupboards. The outdoor one, made entirely of *tolle*, aluminium sheets, is much more interesting to me. The walls and the roof are all made of wavy aluminium sheets too. In fact, apart from the two windows, one on each side and the door, it looks like a big metal box.

"There is an art to making tea Shakti. There is an art to this. Don't you forget this girl!"

"Non Grandpère. mo pas pou blié". I shall not forget

Even though today he is making his special tea for only the two of us as there is no-one else in the house at the moment, Grandpère does not cut corners or skip any of his usual steps. When he comes to pick me up, Daddy will not drink any cold tea. Like him, I like my tea piping hot. It is sacrilege to reheat tea.

I perch myself on a stool a bit away from the gas stove to watch him. I take a big breath in. He is about to start. I am in awe. It is a grandiose ceremony to me. This is a Tea Making Ceremony. An amazing movie is about to start again.

He fills an aluminium pot with fresh cold water from the tap. He lets the water run until he is content with the quantity of water in the pot. This cooking pot is reserved for making tea only. Grandpère would never use this for cooking anything else. No-one in the household would ever dare to go against his directions. He flicks the gas fire on and sets the pot on top of it. He leaves the water to boil gently with the lid off.

"You must not rush the boiling of the water. Never rush the boiling water. Let the water take its time."

"Oui Grandpère.". I respond.

In a small ceramic jug, he mixes two big tablespoons of full cream powdered milk with a little cold water. He swooshes the powder and water with a fork until it turns into a thick paste. He adds a little cold water. Not too much. Not too little. The paste must turn just a little bit like a liquid. Not too runny. Not too thick. He checks the water on the stove. It must be boiled just right. Not hot enough and it will ruin his special tea. Bubbles start to pop. He turns the gas dial all the way to the left until it is off. He bends to flip the clip on the gas tank. He waits.

"You must let the water settle. You want the water to calm down."

I nod.

He stands patiently next to the stove. Content to be still. At ease. A couple of minutes later, he makes his way to the big cupboard full of various boxes and spices. He takes a red box out. I instantly recognise his tea caddy. He keeps the packet of tea leaves in another metal box. This is so that the humidity does not get in and spoil the tea leaves. He does not consider the paper packaging of the tea adequate enough to guarantee the maintenance of its high quality once the packet has been opened. So, he keeps his packet of tea in another sealed metal container.

He scoops two teaspoons of the "*la paille di thé*", the shredded dried leaves of tea, into the now calm hot water. He puts the packet of Bois Cheri Vanilla Tea back in the red metal box and closes the lid. He double checks that it is closed properly.

He puts a lid over the pot of hot water.

He passes me the red box. I open it, bend my head over it and take a big breath in. I adore the aroma of vanilla.

"Ferme li bien" he says. Close it properly.

I double check that I have done so and pass the box back to him.

"Shakti, remember it is crucial to let the hot water settle a little before you add your *la paille di thé*".

"Oui Grandpère", I acquiesce as if I am hearing this instruction for the first time.

"You do not want to spoil the tea leaves. You will spoil the tea leaves if you add them when the water is still boiling."

"Oui Grandpère". I have heard him say this at least a hundred times before.

How can I spoil tea leaves that are already dried and shredded? Maybe dried tea leaves can be damaged. He must be right. He is after all the best tea maker I know. It must be true.

"You do not want to spoil the tea leaves. You want the tea leaves to be perfect. Perfect for your cup of tea."

"Oui Grandpère", I repeat respectfully as a student does to a grand master.

A few minutes later, he lifts the lid and pours the

thick milk liquid over a strainer into the pot. He stirs the content with a long spoon. These too are kept only for tea making. This spoon has never been allowed to touch any curry. The strainer has only ever touched tea. He puts the lid back onto the pot.

"The tea must be covered. It must be allowed to rest. You must give it time to absorb the flavours."

Grandpère walks back into the house to get his magic ingredient from the fridge. He comes back holding an open can of Milkmaid Condensed Milk. He pours some directly from the can into the pot of tea and milk. Another stir with the spoon and the tea is almost ready.

"One final rest. You must give the tea a bit of time to absorb the flavour of the condensed milk too. Everything needs its time. Everything. Remember this girl. Remember this."

"Oui Grandpère".

Yes, I know that things need to take their time

CHAPTER TWENTY-SIX

Family History Comes In Different Forms

"*Ki tasse to lé zordi?*" Which cup would you like today?

These were not ordinary cups or even like the porcelain cups we had to use at Grandma's house or the glass or even china cups I used at other people's houses. These were metal cups. They were kept on the top shelf of the crockery cupboard in the big outdoor kitchen. Ceramic and glass cups were kept in the indoor kitchen. Actually, these metal cups were made of aluminium too; just like the outdoor kitchen.

Grandpère had his own china cup. No-one but he used this. I could choose mine from any of the others. I always discarded the ceramic and glass ones and went straight to the metal ones. Nowhere else had I ever been able to drink tea from metal cups at people's houses. These were no ordinary aluminium cups though. These were part of my family's history; Daddy's family history.

There were thirteen children in Daddy's family.

Please Paint Me Caramel

One more meticulous and set in their ways than the other, and indeed just as temperamental. In order to identify their personal cup, most of them, including Daddy had when they were small dented their cup in their own special way. Thus, they would be able to identify which one was theirs amongst all the other metal cups around.

I once asked Grandpère if he knew which cup belonged to whom. He did not have a clue. I tried to guess which one of my uncles or aunts some cups belonged to depending on their personalities and ways. That did not work! I got Daddy to look among the cups to teach me which ones were for whom of my uncles and aunts. Even though they were quite a few differently bent ones, Daddy confidently picked each cup and stated its owner. Cup after cup he found each owner. He selected thirteen cups and identified thirteen people. One name after another as he picked one cup after another. He was certain. I believed him. This is how I learnt which one was his.

I stand back and scan them. I am looking for a specific one. I know which one I am looking for: Daddy's metal cup from when he was a child. Cup in hand, I turn back to the stove and hand it to Grandpére.

A final stir and he pours the fragrant pale brown liquid through a strainer into my metal cup and his ceramic cup. Two cups of vanilla tea. One for him. One for me.

"*To lé mange kit chose?*" "Would you like something to eat something?" asks Grandpére

"*Mo pas faim*". I am not hungry, I reply

"Did your grandmother tell you not to eat here?"

"*Non. Bien sire ki non!*" I respond indignant.

Grandma had in fact said something derogatory about me stuffing my face with rubbish while I visit him. I was not about to let him know that. There was already enough of a disagreement between the two of them. I was not about to listen to her either.

Grandma in all her mightiness considered herself and her family rank to be far superior to Grandpère's. As often as she deemed fit, she reminded me that I had bad blood running through my veins. I still do not quite understand why it is that it is only I who have any bad blood. Mami's elder sister is married to Daddy's older brother: number 2. They have four children. How come none of the four has any bad blood? How come I am the only one with bad blood? Even though I am the only dark skinned one, I do look like two of them. Surely, they too must have some bad blood!

Grandpère butters a piece of crusty bread for me. He adds some Marmite. He puts the bread on a small side plate and hands it to me.

"*Merci Grandpère*". I thank him as I take a big bite of bread. Crusty bread and Marmite: my favourite too.

I have no intention of missing out. Anyway,

Please Paint Me Caramel

Grandma would never know. I can always lie if she asks me. I can of course have supper twice if need be. I also do not want to upset Grandpère. I know he loves making his special tea for me. He also remembers that I like the crust. This is his way of showing that he somehow cares about me. I can always have supper again at my home later.

CHAPTER TWENTY-SEVEN

Forced Exile

Although they are closer to Sri Lanka and Maldives, the Chagos group of islands belongs to Mauritius. Like all Mauritians I know, I had never been there but I once saw a programme on TV about Diego Garcia, the main island. Beautiful beaches, big palm trees, all kinds of colourful birds and fish were first shown. Then, I saw the deportment of the Chagos people from Diego Garcia to Mauritius.

The British government, to whom Mauritius belonged until its independence in 1968, was loaning Diego Garcia to the United States of America to make a naval base. Mauritius used to be called the key to the Indian Ocean before the Suez Canal was built. I guess Diego Garcia must now be the new key of the Indian Ocean.

Big bags, suitcases and boxes are laden with clothes and other personal belongings. The islanders are not allowed to take everything they own with them; only what they can carry. They have to leave the furniture behind as they are travelling by ship. They nail their homes shut. They barricade

Please Paint Me Caramel

the windows and doors with wooden panels; perhaps to protect against cyclones, perhaps just for peace of mind. The last of the people leave Diego Garcia for Mauritius in 1971.

They walk down the small wooden gangway onto their new promised land one by the one, a few at a time. Some people shout angry protests as they walk past the filming crew. "Forced exile!", they defiantly spit out. Others peacefully walk by shoulders drooping. Still others are crying quietly, some not so quietly.

The faces display various emotions: blank, tired, resigned, desperate, fear. Children mingle among the grown-ups. Their playfulness and faint laughter brutally clash with the rest of the scene. Men and women are close by. There is no laughter from them. No-one smiles.

Mauritius is promised by our government as the land of opportunities. But the reporter also keeps on saying: "Forced exile!"

That television programme was made six years ago. Our living room is quiet. Only Mami and I are watching.

"Forced exile!" the words roll on my tongue. "Forced exile" I repeat confused.

"Why did the Chagos people not want to come live in Mauritius? Why did they not stay to help the Americans? I bet they know a lot about island life: what green plants to eat, where to catch tastier

Shakti Bliss

fish. So many things are poisonous or forbidden! What is forced exile Mami?"

"Slow down girl. So many questions. Slow down" responds Mami

"Why don't they want to come?"

There is a strange tone in Mami voice as she answers my persisting question. She looks sad, very sad. I do not understand why.

"The islanders are not part of the loan. So, they have to leave and come start a new life here" replies Mami; a tired expression on her face. Her tone makes it clear to me that this is the end of that conversation.

"It is time for bed now", she adds a little more animated.

I do not understand why the native people of Chagos had to leave their home. Even I could see a good solution for the islanders, who want to stay, for the islanders who want to leave to have their opportunities and even for the Americans who want their own naval base. I do not understand this forced exile. Surely Diego Garcia can't be that small that it can't even hold the Americans and the Chagos people together in one beautiful place!

Still, so it is. And forced exile, it stays for Jean, Tifi and their people.

CHAPTER TWENTY-EIGHT

The Dance Of People, Fruits And Vegetables

Mami and Daddy were often called *bon dimoune*; good Samaritans. It was not unusual for me to see them get involved with all kinds of different people. I did not know though how Daddy actually got to meet the Chagos community. As he talked to people all the time, maybe he just approached one of them one day.

Whenever I accompanied Daddy anywhere, he routinely stopped every few steps to chat to someone he knew. I had long resorted to not holding his hand but the back of his shirt. This way I could hold on regardless of whether he shook someone's hand or carried woven rattan baskets full of fresh produce. Sometimes though, I got lost. Then all I needed to do was stand where I was and wait for the whistle. Like farmers do with their sheepdogs in English movies, Daddy had a special whistle tune for me. I never stayed lost for long when I was with him. I just had to make my way back to the source of the whistle and there he always was.

The stench of the fish, chicken or meat markets makes me feel nauseous. I wait outside. I try to hold my breath for as long as I can. I breathe through my mouth. I press a handkerchief tightly over my nose. I take quick and shallow breaths to evade the smell. Nothing works. My stomach goes up and down. I try hard not to wretch. No wonder I cannot stand eating any animal or fish.

This part of *Bazar Port-Louis*, the main market of Port-Louis is different. Here among the fruits and vegetables, my stomach settles down. I can breathe. I feel part of something alive. The smells, the colours, the vegetable mongers shouting about their fruits and vegetables intoxicate me. Something grabs my attention. A moment later it is someone else. Then another and, then another.

"Mangues vert, Madame. Joli mangues vert pou faire achard"

Not only do they shout about the green mangoes but they also shout suggestions about what to do with these.

"Letchis bien dou pour faire la bouche content". Sweet litchis to please the mouth.

December, this is litchi season

"Pomme d'amour pour faire rougaille". … Now, something to do with the tomatoes and chutneys…

Fruits and vegetables are piled in neat little or not so little mounds. Some are stacked in baskets, others in big pink, blue, metallic dishes. New, perfect, dented, broken, plastic, metal containers; they are all here. Many colours. Many smells. All together. Yellow pawpaws, red chilies, purple cabbage, stacks of leafy bunches, soil covered potatoes, small round green limes. So many things to see. So many things to eat. Everything sparkles as if polished. All the fruits and vegetables are in full aromatic gear.

CHAPTER TWENTY-NINE

Jean: The Chagos Prince Of Tides

I dart my head in different directions as the calls of the different vendors catch my attention. I love being part of this *meli melo*. I am so enticed by this beautiful ballet of colours and smells as well as people bumping into each other that I do not notice him at first.

Suddenly a few inches from my face, the biggest pair of hands that I have ever seen catch me off guard. My breath jerks in my throat.

I edge behind Daddy clutching the back of his shirt more tightly. I step closer to my father. On the small side for an eight-year-old, my face is level with the two hands. Everything around is buzzing, loud, alive. The two dark hands remain still. They seem to be limply suspended in air. Etiquette forgotten; I stare.

Screened by Daddy's body, I cautiously examine the rest of him. My eyes slowly move up from the hands and take in the muscular arms, the

Please Paint Me Caramel

grey t-shirt, the massive chest and shoulders. He is big. Imposing. Scary to me.

I reach his face. I have never seen a man like this before. I have never seen anyone so black. His skin is so dark that it does not look black or even brown anymore. Instead, it looks almost navy blue. Shiny like a dark fish. He looks like Shaka Zulu, from the movie. But he is even more beautiful than on TV. I stare; all manners and upbringing forgotten.

Vendors and workers are shouting, talking, laughing, banging and engaging in all sorts of activity around us. Customers join in this cacophony. Everybody seems to be moving. He remains poised, unwavering. He stands firm.

I try to follow daddy's conversation with him. He looks like a giant. His soft voice clashes with his big body. He is the most softly spoken man that I have ever heard. His voice is slow. Gentle. Not a whisper. Just soft like warm butterscotch.

I was so busy starring that I had missed the beginning of their conversation.

"That is the land of my ancestors. This is their resting place" he respectfully yet defiantly insists.

"But you can make a good life for yourself here. For your family. A new life for you all" attempts Daddy tagging along with the official slogan we have been brainwashed with.

"Mo pas lé oportunitiés Missier". I do not want opportunities

He pauses. He breathes deeply. He seems to be looking for the right words. He sighs. His lips move but I cannot hear him properly.

"What did you say Jean. I could not hear you" kindly requests Daddy.

I now know his name. Jean.

"That is my home. Diego Garcia is my home"

Daddy, the quick wit usually ever ready with a retort looks on. For the first time in my life, I see him be silent. Jean towers over Daddy. Yet, this massive man now seems smaller. Different. No other word is spoken.

For a couple of seconds, the two men stand facing each other. They are both quiet.

I shift my body so I can see Daddy's face. My eyes quickly turn to Jean again. I do not understand what is going on.

Daddy reaches out and shakes Jean's hand. Holding Jean's big espresso hand in between his pale toffee ones, he murmurs something.

He digs in his shirt pocket for the pen and the list of groceries he keeps there. He tears the bottom of the page, scribbles something. He hands the small piece of paper to Jean.

"Please call me if you ever need any help, Jean. Please call."

Another handshake and we are off.

I do not fully understand about Jean's ancestors' resting place. Are they not reincarnated like my family and me?

Please Paint Me Caramel

Looking over my shoulder as I keep pace with the back of Daddy' shirt, I watch Jean glide away. He is much taller than most of the people around him.

I know. He must be some kind of Prince.

This is when and where I decided that Jean is The Chagos Prince of Tides. Not only because he is like a giant, not because of the way he speaks but because of the way he looks just like black molasses. The molasses which makes the best rum of my country. The molasses that people say can cure the asthma that so many of my relatives are afflicted with. The molasses that makes the best *Tarte Banane*, banana tarts, my favourite sweet cake.

This was the day that I first experienced that black is beautiful.

PART 6

CHAPTER THIRTY

Tifi: Glorious Queen Of Hearts

Life at my home at *37, rue Monsieur* was erratic compared to that of my friends and other people I knew. I called them normal people. There were many moments of excitement alongside the routine of school, play, friends, Grandma's cooking, Mami's reprimands, Daddy's spoils, cousins, uncles, aunts, dogs, cats, Grandma's ducks, her rooster and her pet grouse. Perhaps the most exciting of all was when Tifi exploded in our lives. The moment Tifi landed in my world, I knew that life as I had known it before was never going to be the same again.

A few years after stepping out of the boat from Diego Garcia onto the soil of *Port-Louis* harbour in Mauritius, Tifi, Jean's wife, arrived at my home at *37, rue Monsieur*. To say that this massive woman exploded in my life would be the greatest understatement that I have heard.

Unlike sweet and motherly Lydie, Tifi looked like a big building. She was not fat though. She looked more like a big rectangle on its side. Her knee length and sleeveless dark blue dress with little white and yellow flowers did nothing to soften her appearance or help prevent her from standing out in the front courtyard. The matching scarf tied firmly behind her neck was wrapped so tightly over her hair that it looked as if the whole thing and her head could burst any minute. She held something small in her right hand. I guessed it was her purse.

She waited patiently in front of the big solid wooden door. Behind the closed door, was the road. I don't think that she wanted to run away though; not like me sometimes. She did not look like a person, who ran away. She did not look like a person, who was ever scared of anything.

The dogs, which typically would make a racket whenever someone new came in the yard, had gone silent. This was unheard of. Usually, they would not stop barking viciously whenever someone new or someone they did not like came into the courtyard.

I peep at her from the window in Mami's bedroom. Mami and Daddy's bedroom is right next to the courtyard. I know that it is rude to stare. But I cannot stop. She is the strangest person I have ever seen.

Suddenly, she lifts her head and looks across the yard in the direction of the window. I duck as quickly as I can. Crouching on the floor, my heart is pounding. For a while I stay very quiet; very still. Maybe she has not seen me. Curiosity gets the better of me. I slowly raise my body until my eyes

Please Paint Me Caramel

are just above the windowsill. I try to catch another look at her.

She is looking straight at me.

My face half hidden by the window ledge; I hold her gaze for a few seconds. I am mesmerised by her uniqueness. Alain, my neighbour, who is a few years older than me and as such is very knowledgeable, had told me that the *Illois* dabbled in *gris gris*. *Illois* is what Mauritian people call those from the Chagos islands. *Gris gris* is witchcraft!

Was this woman a *sorcière*? Was she? Was she a witch?

Alain had said that everybody from Diego Garcia practices witchcraft and black magic. I have never seen a *sorcière* before. I also had not heard anyone else say this about the people of Chagos. But I am convinced that she cast a spell on my dogs. Aren't they just staring at her silently instead of barking viciously as they usually do? I had never seen any woman that big before. She must be. She must be a witch.

She is still looking at the place where I am crouching. She looks on as if daring me to stand up. Suddenly she grins at me.

My heart melts. I am filled with warmth. I am bewitched. *Sorcière, gris gris* or whatever else the Chagos people may or may not dabble in, I know that there would be magic in my life.

CHAPTER THIRTY-ONE

The Two Matriarchs

Between Grandma and Mami, it was decided that Tifi would look after the house. Coming to think about it, it was probably Grandma, who had the first as well as the final say in this.

Even though I was still in primary school, I could look after myself fairly well so I did not need my own nanny anymore. I still missed Francès terribly although I knew that she had found a better life in France with her husband. Only on Saturday mornings did Grandma need to help me with oiling my long black hair with coconut oil. This was so that my hair would grow long, silky and thick. Later on, in the morning Mami helped me wash my hair. It was too long for me to be able to do on my own.

The house became Tifi's domain. And her domain, it certainly was!

I did not see Tifi during the week as by the time she arrived in the morning and left in the afternoon, I was at school. Why we had to spend so many hours at school, I did not understand. What a waste of time! If I ever become a minister

Please Paint Me Caramel

in the government, I would shorten school days. Four hours per day, that would be enough! Not six hours per day any longer! Four hours including lunch, tea breaks and play time. As Sundays were her day off, I only got Saturdays and holidays with the glorious Tifi.

In no time, Tifi ruled the house. With a firm *"Madame!"* or a coy *"Mais madame!"*, she would put Grandma in her place when the latter would be complaining about something trivial. Amazingly, out of surprise or dismay, Grandma never even retorted. Instead, she would roll her pale brown eyes, mumble to herself and get on with whatever she was doing. No-one had ever stood up to my Grandma like this before. Yet, there was no insolence or defiance in Tifi's disposition. In fact, I think that these two matriarchs had much respect for one another. Yes, I think Grandma secretly liked Tifi a lot and vice versa. Not that either one of them would ever admit that.

CHAPTER THIRTY-TWO

In The Name Of Beauty

Curlers were one of Tifi's biggest follies in life. She always had a floral headscarf firmly tied on her head like on the first day I saw her. On that day, I thought her head was going to burst. Now I know better.

Different colours of scarf like the different colours of her knee-high floral dresses. Underneath the scarf most of the times, there were big pale pink plastic curlers. I have never actually seen her hair. Once, a curl fell on her forehead. I lifted my hand to gently brush it to the side. Tifi jumped up and rushed to the bathroom, her hand on her hair as she walked away. She spent what seemed to be like an hour in there. When she eventually came out, everything was rigidly tamed, back in the curlers and under the floral headscarf.

I once asked her if she actually slept with them on, *"Ou dormi ek ça?"*

Curtly she said *"Souvent"*. Often!

"Ou pas gagne dimal dans ou li cou?" Don't they hurt your neck?

"*Ou capav dormi ar ça lor ou la tête?*" Can she sleep at all with these on her head?

She laughed at my concern.

"*Ki faire ou mette ça?*" Why do you put these on? I enquired.

"Pou faire zolie!" To make myself beautiful!

"*Zolie couma toi!*". "To be beautiful like you", she chuckled.

Beautiful like me? What? That's a first!

This is the first time that I have heard anyone say that I am beautiful.

I am too stunned to say anything else.

CHAPTER THIRTY-THREE

Saturday Morning Cleaning

Once a month, on the first Saturday of the month actually, it was *grand nettoyage.* For this spring cleaning, the house was cleaned from top to bottom. Everything between the floor and the ceiling would have been cleaned during that week. On the Saturday, it would finally be the turn of the wooden floors in all the rooms. For this grand occasion, on that Saturday morning, everyone would be dispatched from the house. We could linger in the unclean rooms but once Tifi got to them, we had to leave. Only when the entire house was clean and she had gone round and round the rooms to inspect the freshly waxed shining dark brown floors would anyone be allowed in again.

Once Daddy had gone inside a room, which she was cleaning for some reason, which was not deemed important enough by Tifi. Chaos occurred!

"Missieur Daya! Mo pas pou capav travail coume ca!" "Mister Daya, I am not able to work like this!"

Bucket of water, cloths, wax and whatever else

Please Paint Me Caramel

she used to clean, polish and make the floors shine like mirrors were discarded in the middle of the room and she stormed out.

I had never seen her so upset or angry before. I still don't know if she was upset or angry.

It was incredible to watch!

Daddy apologised profusely. Grandma smiled knowingly. The dogs and I watched intently and Mami coaxed her gently. Eventually with a big sign, which seemed to come from the bottom of her stomach, Tifi got up from the stone steps in front of the house, on which she had planted herself solidly.

"Juste pou ou Madame Daya, juste pou ou!"
"Only for you Madame Daya, only for you".

Tifi had a special fondness for Mami, whom she called *Madame Daya.* I had not heard anyone call Mami by my father's name before or since. Daddy was *Missieur*, Mister in Creole. Grandma was *Madame* and me: *Fi* (little girl) or *Ma fi* (my little girl) depending on her mood and her level of fondness for me. Coming to think about it, she never ever called me by my name. When I went to her place, then I became *mo bourgeois so tifi*; the daughter of my master.

I never understood why she would on such occasions call me "the daughter of my master". Everyone knew that nobody was Tifi's master! Not even Daddy whom on such occasions she insisted on calling her master. It was weird to hear my father called that. It was like the slaves used to call their owners! No matter what Daddy said, she carried on. So, he eventually got used to being called *"mo bourgeois"* no matter how uncomfortable this evidently made him feel.

Yet again only Mami's words seemed to be able to appease Tifi. She eventually went back inside to carry on with what she had been doing.

Everyone glared at Daddy, including the dogs. He did not go inside to disturb Tifi's cleaning ever again.

CHAPTER THIRTY-FOUR

Respect and The Fisherman's Catch

Tifi lived in Cassis. This used to be part of crown land but the government had given the people of Chagos some land on which they could build their houses. There, a row of lovely aluminium or tin houses was swiftly built.

Jean, Tifi's husband, the most beautiful man and the closest look-alike to Shaka Zulu I knew, worked on the docks. He carried bags of sugar on his back onto the ships. But he also had another job. He was a *pêcheur.* As a fisherman, he would seek *crevettes (*prawns) and *chevrettes* (shrimps) as well as fish of course. Sometimes he would make special trips to catch *camaron* (lobster) and *ourite* (octopus). Well, in brief, he caught all the things that Mami and Daddy absolutely adored, but to which I had been allergic since I was a baby. An old aunt once said that I was allergic to seafood because Mami ate too much of it when she was pregnant with me. In my family, such explanations made perfect sense.

Shakti Bliss

Although being a *pêcheur* was not his main work, as Daddy often commented to all those he knew, Jean was a very good fisherman so it was only right for us to give him a very good price for his catch. This is a good opportunity for Jean to make extra money.

Although I personally didn't like the smell or the look of these creatures, I was fond of both Jean and Tifi so I never missed the opportunity to go to their place whenever Daddy went to fetch the catch. However, it was much more of a complex activity than me simply sitting in the car on a Sunday afternoon.

On the day before, Tifi would choose a dress for me. Before the first trip, I was given a thorough examination and summed up as:

"Ou en pe brune! Mais pas faire nannien!" "You are bit dark. Never mind!"

So, it was concluded that I am a little on the dark side. But at least, it did not bother her too much. What a relief!

Mami sorted my clothes for the washing machine but as Tifi ironed all my clothes, she probably knew them better than I did. The day before my visit, Tifi would select what I would wear on the following day. She was actually not in charge of my clothes. I usually chose what I wanted to wear except for when we went visiting relatives or attended special events like weddings. Then, Mami made sure that I was in perfect attire. She said it had to do with *honneur.* I did not understand what the family's honour had to do with my dresses. Visiting Tifi was not considered such an important occasion by Mami but to Tifi and to me, it most certainly was.

Tifi not only sorted out my dress but hair clips and shoes too. Once, she even stayed overtime to clean and polish my shoes. She would even discuss my hairstyle with me: plaits, ponytail, pig tails, loose … What is it going to be this time? I had to be perfect! Just perfect!

Once I ran out of time because of playing and jumped into the car as I was. When we arrived in front of her house, Tifi took one look at me and left me in the car. Jean and Daddy were so busy sorting out the catch and money that they did not even notice that I had been left alone. She did not speak to me for two whole Saturdays after that. Only when I apologised, did we go back to being friends. I never dared go visit her at her home ever again without looking perfect. To Tifi, me visiting her was much more than a mere social call, and I only showed disrespect to her that one time.

I sure needed her on my side. With one swift *"ou pou pleuré kan li alle aprane dehors"*, she would remind Mami in the midst of her reprimanding me about something or another, that Mami would miss me and cry for me when I go to study overseas. Of course, I could not afford to get Tifi upset with me. She was a very good protector. She would even stand up to Grandma for me.

CHAPTER THIRTY-FIVE

The Grand Tour Of The Illois Community

Tifi's house was next to the street. As soon as Daddy's car stopped, she would be there on the pavement. I don't think that she had been actually waiting for us there but I am sure that she had some kind of system going. Of course, Daddy would be regimental about being there on time to meet Jean as Tifi had planned.

As we went through the same ritual every time, I had very quickly learnt the twists and turns of those visits.

"Bonjour Jean"

"Bonjour mamzelle", replied the ever-courteous Jean. To him, I was a *mademoiselle*, a young lady. *Mamzelle* for short.

"Bonjour Tifi"

Bon, mumbles Tifi inspecting me from head to toe, then working her way back upwards again. Sweeping off some non-existent fluff from my hair, she straightens my already well pressed dress.

Even though Tifi's house is right next to the

Please Paint Me Caramel

street, we go on what I can only refer to as a grand tour of Cassis before we actually get to her shiny and warm metal house.

"Bonjour Denise"

"*Zenfant mo bourgeois ça*". "This is my master's child".

If whoever was outside their house, I would be introduced yet again, not by my name as is usually done by all Mauritians I knew, but as "the child of my master". How funny! Funny, because although Daddy paid Tifi's wages, I think that she was more of his *bourgeois*, than the other way round. Still, I suppose to the outside world, he was Tifi's boss.

If Solange was in her house or out of sight, then a different scenario was performed.

"*Solange, Solange, Solange, kotte ou?*" bellows Tifi at the top of her voice.

"*Ah, ou la! Zenfant mo bourgeois ti envi trouve ou!*"

When on earth did I ever say to Tifi that I wanted to see Solange? But of course, far from me the madness to retort. Instead, beaming I would promptly add:

"*Bonjour!*"

In the early days, I used to say: "*Bonjour Madame!*"

I got severely reprimanded by Tifi.

When I said, "*Bonjour Solange*" or "*Bonjour Denise*" or whoever it was, this was not allowed either. I have to simply say "*Bonjour!*" But I could smile as brightly as I wanted. Tifi explained that it had something to do with my standing, my status. Smiling was acceptable.

"Mo ene zenfant! Zotte grand dimoune!" I answered back indignant. I sometimes could not help myself. Indeed, I was a child and her neighbours Solange and Denise were grown-ups.

Responding to my confusion, Tifi then patiently yet with one sentence explained the situation to me:

"To famille mo bourgeois. Donc, to superieur!"

I was dazzled and even more confused by her explanation. I understood the part about my family being her boss and employing her, but nobody had ever called me superior before!

Hmmm! That's new to me!!

Of course, we never stayed long in front of anyone's house. She most certainly never allowed me to go inside anyone else's home. Instead, she dismissed any invitation with a firm *"mo bourgeois préssé"*. Needless to admit that Daddy had in fact never ever said that he was in a hurry. He would not have dared to say something like that to Tifi.

After the grand tour of what seems to be the entire *Illois* community in Cassis, we finally get to Tifi's house, her beaming, me exhausted and eager for the big glass of the special *jus tamarin*, which she would joyfully make for me from fresh Tamarind pulp, brown sugar and cold water. Nowhere else in the world does Tamarind juice taste as delicious as it does in Tifi's aluminium house.

Jus tamarin aside, Tifi's words "*to superieur*" lingers in my mind.

"Superieur? Moi?" Me? Hmmm…

No one had ever called me superior before. In my family, I was definitely not superior. This is why I wanted to be caramel… to be like the others… Not inferior anymore!

Maybe it did not matter then that I am not caramel.

Maybe that's just Grandma's problem with me.

Maybe… maybe… all I need to do is to go live somewhere where I am *superieur*!

Hmmm… something to think about….

PART 7

CHAPTER THIRTY-SIX

Praised Be The Goddess

I try hard to keep Grandma in sight. I feel like holding on to her saree like I used to try to do when I was a little girl. She says it is common to hold on to someone's clothes. I know I am not allowed to get lost. Not today. I shall never be able to find her again among all these people.

The entire Tamil population of the island seems to have turned up at the temple in *Terre Rouge*. I wish Grandma had chosen a bright-coloured saree. Bright colours abound here. I think no-one is allowed to dress in black in the temples, at least not for the women. Men can wear black trousers. I don't think that I have ever seen a man in a black shirt though. I don't know if long black skirts are allowed for teenagers. I don't think so. I don't recall having seen any of my friends or cousins wear long black skirts at the temples. I also have not worn any. It would have been so much easier for me to keep track of her in the crowd if she wore something sparkling too. Being a widow, she only wears dark demure colours.

A woman's voice is singing devotional prayers. I cannot see her. I can only hear her because she is using a microphone. The sound of harmonium, tablas, a type of Indian drum, and timbales add to the harmonious melodies. It is hard for me to concentrate. The smell of burning camphor tickles my nostrils and clears my already unobstructed sinuses. The menthol blisters away any potential cold that could be lurking in my imminent karma. As soon as I start showing signs of a cold, Grandma wraps a piece of camphor in the corner of a clean white handkerchief and ties it around my left wrist, directly on my pulse. She keeps doing so every night until the cold is completely gone. This not only induces deep sleep but also obliterates all symptoms of the ailment. Camphor is both sedative and anti-bacterial.

The chime of the brass bell brings me back to the here and now. I move my legs a little. It is hard to sit still and cross-legged on the floor for so long.

"Arrète bougé! To pas capav assise en place?" 'Stop moving. Can't you sit still?" scolds Grandma.

My knee stops in mid-air. I do not answer back. We are after all in front of the shrine of the goddess.

The priests continue to conduct *avshyom* and *archaneys*, special prayers inside the inner temple where the main shrine stands. Only they are allowed in that area. Mere morals, like Grandma and me, are not allowed to touch the *murti*. Everybody

Please Paint Me Caramel

knows this. Everybody respects this. The *murti*, the statue must be kept pure.

Murtis are mostly made of black stone. They must be sculpted from only one block of stone or rock. How can they make such intricate sculptures from just one piece of stone? This is the rule. All *murtis* for the Tamil temples are made in India from sacred quarries. I wonder if there is only one sacred quarry or more. I think there must be more than one as there are so many stone *murtis* sent all over the world. They are all made in South India. Must the sculptors come from the same family lineage or can anyone become a sculptor of *murtis*? *Murtis* are also made of metal. They often look like gold to me but I don't know if it is solid gold; perhaps brass. Sometimes they look golden. Sometimes they look silvery. I think some *murtis* are also made of ceramic or clay. This is how they can be painted in vibrant colours; white face and pink cheeks. I have never seen a *murti* painted the same colour as my face and arms. This statue of the deity is made of black stone.

People bring their trays of fruits, incense sticks, milk or other offerings for the goddess. Some pilgrims bring sarees. We all also put some money in the metal donation boxes. Devotees are here to ask for blessings, in gratitude, or whatever else is considered appropriate reason. There is no set reason. There is no set formula. One purpose

Shakti Bliss

unites us. We are all here in reverence to the goddess.

The singing stops. The music stops.

The head priest, the *ayer*, starts chanting prayers. The other younger priest passes him one *sombu* after another. The head priest looks much older than his assistant. Each brass container reveals a different liquid. He pours a golden yellow liquid on the top of the deity's head and on the rest of her frame. This is a mix of water and turmeric. It is to cleanse her. This is the same mixture that is used during weddings too. I think it is also used to bathe children when they have measles. The liquid flows down onto her body. Some splash him. He pours milk on her head and over her. His gestures are slow, reverent. The white liquid glides over the blackness of the sculpture. Last, he pours a *sombu* of water slowly all over her and behind her too. His arms, hands and fingers move in graceful waves over and around the goddess. Yet, they never touch her. He sweeps away the water at the bottom of her feet with his hands.

The young priest draws the curtain closed. The curtain in front of the inner sanctum keeps the rest of the procedures even more sacred. The four priests in the inner temple carry on with the rest of the sacred procedures untarnished by our impure eyes.

The music resumes. The singing woman joins in.

Please Paint Me Caramel

I catch sight of the young guy in the white shirt. He is staring at me again. I do not know him personally but I have seen him before. I have also seen him looking at me before. Temples and weddings are prime ground for meeting potential spouses and a wife for one's son, grandson or relative. He is quite good looking but I have no interest in him; not today. I am not being coy. Grandma would strangle if she caught on to his interest. As for me, I have much more important things on my mind today. I avert my eyes and pretend not to notice him.

Grandma is as stoic as ever. When I look more closely, I notice that she too is moved by what is going on. Beads of perspiration are gathering on her temples. A droplet escapes down her plump cheek. Her usually fair face is flushed pink. I am not sure if it is from the heat, the crowd sitting so close together or the significance of this ceremony. Maybe it is something else. I watch her intently. Her lips press firmly against each other. She turns her head away from me.

I think about her life, the hardships which she almost never ever refers to. I wonder what she prays for. Does she still think about how scared she was when she got married at twelve years old? Has she forgiven her mother for how betrayed she felt when she learnt that she had been promised for marriage to that older man when she was only six years old? Does she remember how difficult it was to adjust to the husband's family? Does she still think about the still born baby she had when she was twenty-four years old? Does she ever get angry with God that her healthy four-year old child caught polio and became physically handicapped overnight? Does she still think about her husband, who died suddenly when she was only thirty-three? Has she forgotten about how her mother-in-law completely trampled and dominated her? What does she long for? What does she pray for?

The singing and harmonious music suddenly stop. *Tappus*, the devotional drums, pound a deafening rhythm. Loud, louder, louder still. The *morlums*, a kind of Indian clarinet like the ones Cobra charmers use, squeak their way in. Everything is at full volume. Maximum power.

The curtain opens.

CHAPTER THIRTY-SEVEN

Fire Walking At The Kali Temple

Four men are playing traditional instruments reserved for religious festivals. Two are beating *tappus*. These circular drums are similar to the ones played by the Irish. With their left hand they hold the *tappu* as they walk. In their right hand, they hold a stick with which they beat the drum. Another two men are playing the *morlums*. Do they intend to mesmerise us like Cobra charmers do to the snake? They are all dressed in *vestis*, white cotton sarongs, and plain cotton short-sleeved shirts. One is in a blue shirt, two in white shirts and the other in a brown one. Only men from special family lines are allowed to play these instruments for the religious festivals. It is an unwritten rule. Like so much, nothing is written about this. Together these sounds add more to the cacophony around than resemble any music. There is no harmonious tune. There is no word. There is no apparent script. The men either beat or blow. Hard. Loudly.

I join the crowd's response. After each verse,

we shout "Om Shakti", Hail to the Goddess Shakti, the Goddess Mother.

My heart pounds in unison with the beat of the *tappus*. The sounds pull my attention in different directions. Each instrument follows its own symphony. Yet, there is a wholeness. They somehow belong together like a jazz band. Underneath each stream of sound, there is a rhythm. The men are beating the *tappus* and blowing the *morlums* to attract the attention of a specific goddess. They are calling her. They are charming her to come to us, the devotees. She is Maha Kali: Kali the great one. She is also sometimes called Kali Mai or Kali Ma: Mother Kali.

The effect on the devotees all around me is potent but as all things in Tamil celebrations varied. Some sway joyfully aligning their soul's rhythm to that of the musical instruments. One *tappu*? Two *morlums*? All of them? Who knows, specificity is irrelevant here. Many people pray fervently: loudly, quietly; each in their own time; each in their own way. I don't try to eavesdrop. This is sacred. This is private. This is between them and the Shakti.

The smoke from the sandalwood incense sticks mingles with the green acrid smell of the *Leela* leaves, neem leaves, which are used for purification. *Leela* is the symbolic leaf for the Shakti, the Goddess Mother. *Leela* leaves are also used in water to help cleanse children when they have measles. It is known to be a powerful disinfectant.

Please Paint Me Caramel

The distinct sweet or citrus smells of the various flowers add different perfume notes. The ensemble of aromas is intoxicating and assaulting.

Many people go into trance. They move in their distinct way: gently, harshly and erratically. Some in their own form of dance. People with eyes closed, people with eyes wide open. I am no longer scared of the people in trance. Grandma explained to me that this is just how the soul of the people needs to express their devotion to the goddess. Each person is expressing their connection to her. It is the language of their sacred union with the goddess.

Suddenly something brushes down my right arm. The middle-aged woman next to me is on her knees. Her bun becomes loose as she shakes her head violently from side to side. Her long black hair cascades over her shoulders and gets all tangled up. The standing crowd promptly parts to give her more space. She is sobbing crouched almost on the ground. A few minutes later, an old woman steps forward. Bending down, she lifts the younger woman's wet face and presses some sacred ash on her third eye. Within minutes she calms down. She stays on her knees a while longer. Slowly she gathers her saree around her ankles and stands up. Nobody stares. She carries on with her prayers holding her *mundani*, the front of her saree, wide open in front of her body. Heart open. Praying for solace with all her might.

The firewalking starts. Several priests go first as they complete many offerings. One by one what seems like hundreds of firewalkers walk in the pit still full of burning coals and embers. Some walk fast, some slowly, some very slowly. Only very few run. At the end of the fire pit, they dip their feet in another pit dug into the soil. Grandma has donated the milk to fill that pit and cool the feet of the firewalkers. An ornate and painted statue of Maha Kali sits high on a specially set shrine right in front of the milk. She is there so that the firewalkers may look straight at her as they walk on the sacred fire. She is not black here but is like her other sisters Durga, Lutchmee and Saraswati. Once again, she is dressed in a colourful saree and is adorned with gold jewels and flowers. Here she looks exactly like them. Her face is fair and she is smiling.

"*Vini*", directs Grandma as she pulls my arm. "Come"

"*Non. Mo pas encore finie*". "No, I am not ready to leave yet", I say firmly but as respectfully as I can muster.

Grandma looks up puzzled. She remains sitting.

Without another word, I turn away from her and make my way closer to the goddess.

"*Attene moi ici. Mo vini la*". "Wait for here. I am coming back soon".

My hand lightly leans on the shoulder of the old lady sitting on the floor in front of us. The silk cloth of her saree comes to meet my skin in a gentle, soft yet firm way. The cloth is unsteady under my palm at first. Then, as if mimicking how I am feeling, the silk pleated folds become steadier under my grip as I hold on a little more boldly. I press a little harder. Keeping my balance one footstep at a time and tip toeing, I sleekly make my way in between the praying and watchful devotees. We are all putting our trust in Maha Kali.

I keep going closer and closer. I will not stop. I have a plan.

CHAPTER THIRTY-EIGHT

Even Hindu Deities Are Fair

My mind is lured away by the aromas, the heat and my own devotion. I feel light-headed. My heart is beating so fast that it might jump out from under my *salwar kamiz*.

At fourteen, I am too young to wear a saree to come to the temple but as I have already started menstruating, Grandma says that my regular knee length dresses are no longer suitable for special festivals. Instead, I am now kitted in a pair of pale blue loose cotton trousers. The matching dress falls below my knee. Pale blue is considered adequate for my dark skin. The embroidered transparent long light pashmina, *horni*, draped over my left shoulder adds a touch of feminine finesse. Tamil women wear the top of their saree on the left shoulder. So, teenagers and girls also do so with their *hornis*. The same gold and turquoise blue delicate embroidery pattern lines the bottom of my dress, the bottom of my trousers and the four edges of the scarf. As Mami said this morning when she checked me before I left the house, I look respectable for the

Please Paint Me Caramel

temple. Mami does not come here. It is too intense for her. Daddy brought us by car and dropped us off this morning. He is a devotee of another deity, another aspect of God.

The sounds are so loud that they go right through my body. They resonate in me. I feel every vibration. It feels like an earthquake in my body. I close my eyes to savour this sacred moment. Every cell of my body soaks the specialness of this occasion. Sacred, doubly sacred. Today is my favourite day after my birthday. Today we are celebrating my favourite goddess, Kali Ma.

Shush! I am not allowed to say this out loud. Grandma says that no maiden and girl should be a devotee of Kali as she has a fighting spirit and is not good for marriage. With my slimmer chances even with my prestigious family name to get a good husband compared to my cousins, I am not allowed to risk openly having that kind of disposition. I already often get into trouble for always answering back and wanting to do things my way.

Grandma responsibly has been manoeuvring me towards devotion to the other main goddess sisters. *Durga*, the deity who represents the motherhood aspect of God is recommended as she is also good to help make healthy babies. She is very popular with married women and those on the lookout for a good spouse. *Lutchmee*, the bountiful or provider deity bestows wealth and abundance of material and spiritual nature, is equally strongly recommended for me. She could help me get some beauty; a sure asset to lure a good husband. *Saraswati*, the source of all learning and knowledge of arts and music, would be good for my studies. If on the looks front, I am no match for others at least my intellect could be my strength. There! Different deities to suit your specific needs! Grandma considers *Saraswati* to be best suited for me. So, she has made a gold pendant of *Saraswati* for me to wear around my neck.

I mean no disrespect to any of these deities. They are all fair and beautiful. I am sure that they are very powerful too. I am well aware that I could do with some help from all of them. They do not draw me though. I so wish that I could feel differently. I so wish that I could be like my other cousins.

Kali, on the contrary, captivates my imagination. She is like a magnet to my heart. Kali is the divine aspect, which is responsible for the destruction and eradication of negative qualities in the world. I have only recently read about this. But I have loved her since I was a little girl. I call her Kali Ma. I had to keep this a secret though. I still do.

As the divine aspect responsible for the destruction of negativity, she is one of the most fearsome of the expressions of divinity in Hinduism. However, she does not scare me. Not at all. Not anymore that it is. When I was younger, I can't remember exactly how old but a long time ago, I

Please Paint Me Caramel

used to get confused by her red tongue sticking out. The fact that she had one foot on top of someone lying on the ground baffled me. I was horrified when I learnt that it was Shiva, Lord of the Universe. But what really worried me was the garland of bloodied heads around her neck. There are no bodies attached to those heads and their eyes are all still wide open!

Grandma explained that *Kali* had been created from *Durga* to destroy the demons that had been plaguing the universe. The garland was made of the heads of those demons. When she was cutting the heads of the demons in the fight, as their blood hit the ground, ten more rose from each drop of blood. She had to lick the blood before it fell to the ground so no more demons could be created. This is the reason why her tongue is red and is sticking out. It makes perfect sense. She was the saviour; a protector. That is why she needed to be vicious. She was fighting demons. She did what she had to do.

It is a bit like when Krishna and Alain annoy me. As I am much smaller than them, I cannot fight them off by force alone. So, I dig my nails deep into their arms or wherever I can reach and scratch. Of course, I get into trouble for hurting them and sometimes drawing blood. But it works and they do leave me alone. Even though Mami and Grandma hit me afterwards and make me apologise to them, I am not always really sorry.

Sometimes though when I scratch them too badly, I feel awful afterwards. I then pray for their wounds to heal quickly. I do what I have to do, just like Kali.

I cannot remember since when I have felt so drawn to Kali. I feel very close to her. Connected. But I can't say this to anybody. No-one in my family knows. It is my secret.

Perhaps I feel this way because unlike the other female deities, who are all fair skinned, she is portrayed as black. She is called as dark as the moonless night in the sacred books. Yes, unlike every other female deities in the Hindu mythology, she is the only dark one.

Even though she is often portrayed as looking horrible, I feel that she understands me. Yes, she too knows how it feels to look different on the outside. I bet she knows how it feels to look different from all the others in her family too. She knows how hard it is to be dark skinned in an Indian family.

CHAPTER THIRTY-NINE

Yellow is the colour. Bliss is the way

Seven in the afternoon, the fire walking is over. It is almost dark outside. This is the last phase of the celebration of Maha Kali. We are inside the temple to give thanks to the goddess for her protection of all the firewalkers as well as the *cavadee* and *pal kodhum* bearers earlier that morning. They are all dressed in yellow. All their clothes have been put in *de l'eau saffron*, turmeric water too, to purify them before they wore these today. They have all been fasting for ten days like Grandma and me. Yellow is the colour of the Goddess Mother on my island. There is relief in the air. The devotion and gratitude are even stronger.

I am sitting cross-legged on the floor. Next to me, Grandma looks tired. She looks old. We have been here since nine in the morning. She woke up at five to wash her hair to purify herself before coming to the temple. As an old woman, she is not allowed to leave her hair open so she needed time for it to dry before tying it in her usual bun. She

Shakti Bliss

refuses to use a hair dryer. I just let mine loose to dry after I wash it.

We are on the women's side. Men and women sit separately. I don't know why. Perhaps it is so we don't get tempted by each other. That is how it is at temples. Women sit on the floor in the main area. Men are at the back and on the left side. Very old people are on the few chairs, which are available. Young boys are allowed to stay with their mothers. As usual, Grandma and I have excellent seats near the front. We all sit close to each other to allow as many people as possible to be inside the temple. Thankfully the open terraced area allows some fresh air to circulate. There are no fans here. There is also no health and safety regulation about any maximum number of people to be allowed in.

The priest is performing the *arthi*, the reverence ceremony. The lit camphor cubes at the end of the elongated small brass tray spits. I follow the flame with my eyes. In clockwise movements, he circles the front of the goddess. First the camphor, then incense sticks. This is followed by an array of different religious artifices. All of which are considered her weapons and fares. The stone statue of the goddess is now dressed in a beautiful gold and green sari. She is heavily adorned with solid gold jewellery. There is no costume jewellery or plated gold embellishments here. With her two ornately designed necklaces and heavy bangles on both hands, she looks prosperous. The thick gold

Please Paint Me Caramel

necklaces glitter against the camphor flame. Her adornments and bright saree make her sparkle. Another light is switched on dissipating in a second the natural darkness of the inner temple. Electricity elevates the sacredness of the inner temple too.

Quietly so Grandma won't hear me, I pray. For me, as usual it is no prayer of gratitude or penance. Of course, I know many mantras by heart. I can rattle one hundred and eight Gayatri mantras without a break. Instead, it's my usual plea. Six words over and over: "Please paint me caramel Maha Kali". As there is a rule in Hinduism that there must be no taking without giving, in exchange I promise to be good. I change my promise: "I shall try to be good Maha Kali". One must never break a promise to God.

Head bowed, palms touching and eyes closed, I focus on my prayer. Suddenly something softly touches the top of my head, right on my crown chakra. I jerk my head up as my hand reaches for the spot brushing anything from the top of my head. There is nothing. I scoop my hair to one side to check if any insect has fallen on me. Both Krishna and Alain have told me that lizards sometimes fall off the ceiling onto the heads of people. There is nothing in my hair either. I glance at my clothes to check if anything could be lurking there. Nothing. I tilt my head back to look at the ceiling. There is no sight of any lizard there.

I close my eyes again. I feel a strange sensation

in my head. My body feels tense but my head feels light. I am still a bit anxious about the possible insect or lizard. A lizard falling on your head brings bad luck. Within a few seconds, this feeling spreads from my head down my neck, chest to the rest of my body. I feel completely light. I cannot feel any part of my body. Eyes heavy. I close them tighter. My mind wonders. Am I levitating like the yogis I have seen on television? I do not dare open my eyes to check in case the feeling goes away. Anyway, I don't care. This feels good. I'll deal with any repercussion later.

I surrender to the comfort. It feels as if I am burying myself completely into a soft cushion. A warm gentle breeze surrounds me. It envelops me in a cocoon. I am wrapped by a fluffy cloud. I take a deep breath, slowly. I savour the feeling. The bells and the priest's voice are distant, muffled. I feel lighter and lighter.

I am in a kind of still trance. Everything appears to be in slow motion. Everything is a little blurred. Gently, I lower my almost closed eyes to my hands. They are lying limply in my lap. They look different. They appear to be surrounded by a kind of thin golden cloud. Is this my aura that I see?

Something stirs in the middle of my solar plexus, near the pit of my stomach. It is like the build-up for the eruption of a volcano. I am a little nauseous. The whirling circle in the middle of my abdomen gets bigger and bigger. It engulfs my chest, my

Please Paint Me Caramel

shoulders, my entire body. My eyes fling open. My body tingles all over. I shiver. My breathing is erratic. I close my eyes again. I try to calm myself down. Breathe in deeply, deeply, deeply.

    I sigh in bliss. My heart swells. A tear spills from my right eye.

CHAPTER FORTY

The Gift Of My Heart

"*Shakti, nou allé!*" "Shakti, we are leaving!"

"*Shakti! Vini!*" says the sound louder. "Shakti! Come!".

Grandma voice jerks me out of my bliss.

"*Sept heures et demi passé. To papa pou là pou vine cherche nou. Degagez!*" "It is past seven thirty. Your father will be here to collect us. Hurry up!".

Slowly the cold and hard ground under me becomes more obvious. I slightly open my eyes and look at the goddess a few metres in front of me. I gaze at Maha Kali. I close my eyes again. I take another deep breath. I want to wait for the moment when the head priest will blow in the conch, the sacred shell. This is my favourite moment of any ceremony at the temple.

"*Shakti!*"

"*Shakti!*"

I refuse to hurry up. I gently straighten the scarf back onto my left shoulder and pull my dress in order. I kneel to bow in respect. Touching the cold concrete floor with my forehead is soothing. I linger there longer than usual.

As I stand up, I stumble. I hold on to the shoulder of the lady in front of me to catch myself from falling over her. My legs feel like jelly. My body is numb. I manoeuvre my way through the sitting ladies and children avoiding legs and bodies as I gingerly head to the exit.

As I turn to bow to Kali before stepping out of the front section of the temple, a big yellow marigold falls from the garland of flowers around her neck. My heart explodes. My face lights up. It is for me. I know it is for me. It is not possible for me to go tell the priest this and collect my gift. I know that. It does not matter. I know that the flower is for me. This is what is most important.

"*Merci*", I grin a silent inner "Thank You"

A hundred more excuse me's later, exhausted from holding back my exhilaration and avoiding stepping on anyone's legs, I am finally at the back of the temple.

"*Shakti! Vini donc!*" "Shakti! Come along", snaps Grandma.

Suddenly, she stops in her forceful track and stares at me.

"*Ki to gagné?*". "What is wrong with you?"

Nothing, I answer coyly as I turn my head and wink at the Kali Ma, my Kali Mai.

EPILOGUE

More than thirty years have passed since that day at the Firewalking festival in Terre Rouge.

Some days I see myself fairer in the mirror. Some days I see myself darker in the same mirror. Some days I catch myself wishing that I am fairer like my cousins are. On other days, it does not matter to me. I have stopped wearing pastel colours. Instead, most of my clothes are now red.

Around me my community, culture and family still value fairness. The Shaadi.com dating website aimed at Indians and people of Indian descent still asks about one's skin colour and the colour of one's preference in a partner. Options are offered. It is like a multiple-choice question we are asked during an exam. The cover of magazines and editorial photographs enforce this.

Fair still means more beautiful. Sometimes I think so too. Sometimes I don't. Still, what I strive to do is to value myself: my assets, my strengths, my uniqueness. Me. All of me.

With my grey hairs poking out from underneath the thick black ones, I have understood that Butterscotch, Fudge, Syrup, Toffee, Treacle, Molasses, we are all simply Caramel. Cooked sugar. Variations of cooked sugar. *Café au Lait*,

Cinnamon, Chocolate, Coffee, *Dulce de Leche*, Mocha. We are all delicious.

That's all it is. Delicious. All of us, delicious in our own way.

Om Shakti
Hail to all the Goddesses treading
this earth and beyond
Hail to all little baby girls, young girls,
teenagers, women, elders
Hail to all of us
Hail to all our Shades of Caramel

ACKNOWLEDGEMENTS

A special thank you to Mark and his writing groups of 2005 and 2006 at Ottakar's and Waterstones, whose curiosity and enthusiasm kindled me to start writing this novel and to continue to tell the stories of my childhood. Thank you dear peers for seeing the kind of author I was and that I am long before I did. Yes, I started writing Please Paint Me Caramel in 2005. It took me until 2023 to muster the courage to let it be visible to the world. It took me until 2023 to muster the courage to let these parts of me be known by others. Yes, this too is me. Yes, it has been 18 years. It is time.

Thank you to Jackee, Courttia, Will, Linda Joy and my many teachers, who over the years showed me the craft of writing. Thank you to the members of the Writing Group in Forres, Scotland, in particular Tez and Andy, who have welcomed me with my quirkiness and different perspectives from another part of the world. Thank you to all those, who have helped me believe in myself as an author. You know who you are. Thank you to Tricia and Andrew, who would not let me forget that I wanted to be an author and help make a difference.

Thank you to those, who have seen my strength and courage when I could not. Thank you to those, who have believed in me long before I did and who continued to do so when I did not. Thank you to those, who have loved me. Thank you to those, whom I have loved.

Above all, thank you to the little girl that I was. Wow! What a girl!! I am in awe of you dearest. I so long for your faith, courage and sparkle.

Apologies to anyone, whom I may have forgotten.

Thank you.

MORE PLEASE PAINT ME ...

Dear readers,

Have you experienced colourism? I would love to hear your stories about colourism and your skin colour. I would love to publish your stories in an anthology. Would you like to contribute your story? I believe that together we can help heal each other as well as help change devaluing mindsets and behaviours.

Stories may be up to 1200 words. You may submit an original story, poem or even drawing to illustrate the difficulties you have encountered with regard to colourism or the colour of your skin. I shall ensure that you are credited and acknowledged for your submission. Please respect copyright guidelines.

Just send a copy of what you would like to contribute to the following email address:

shakti@shaktibliss.org

In the subject field, please put: Contribution - Please paint me

If in doubt about what you would like to contribute, please contact me.

Together we can help heal each other and help change devaluing mindsets and behaviours; including our own.

As Lucinda from the group Bliss sings in Break The Chain,

> *"...Who's gonna make the change?
> Who's gonna lead the way?..."*

Thank you for breaking the chain

Shakti x

WHO IS SHAKTI?

Shakti is a non-fiction author, poet and photographer focusing on empowerment, in particular girls and women empowerment. She has been part of the Women of the World Conference, One Billion Rising and a supporter of PAWA, Rising Woman Rising World.

Like Nelson Mandela, whom she heard say: *"if you want to change the world, change education"*, she believes in the power of education whether formal or informal, structured or unstructured, to help raise awareness about persisting difficulties. She believes that such education can help create better futures, communities and societies. The ultimate aim of her work is inner leadership and self-mastery.

She is an educator, workshop leader and consultant specialising in Wellbeing, Authentic Branding and Communications. She thoroughly enjoys leading yoga Nidra, deep relaxation and meditation/ contemplation sessions. She has participated in and led social projects as well as educational projects in several languages and countries. She adores participating in or leading women's sharing circles such as the Red Tent. She is fluent in five languages including English, French and Spanish. She works in several languages. She loves working with individuals, groups as well as organisations. She strives to include all stakeholders' experiences and perspectives. She believes that together we can create better solutions.

She is increasingly integrating the varied parts of her character and personality. She is becoming more and more honest about her identity and facets. She is discovering and exploring her own authenticity and power as she increasingly follows an inside out perspective. She is learning and blossoming, albeit slowly; too slowly she sometimes thinks.

As Polonius advises his son Laertes in Shakespeare's Hamlet:

> *"This above all: to thine own self be true. And it must follow, as the night the day, Thou canst not then be false to any man".*

She has often stumbled but keeps on getting up and dusting herself off. She holds on to her belief in a happy and safe life.

For information about speaking engagements, other books, audio content, exhibitions, workshops and training programmes, please send an email to:
shakti@shaktibliss.org
In the subject field, please put: More information about Shakti.

OTHER NON-FICTION FROM SHAKTI

BOOKS:

Please Paint Me Caramel *(debut novel and the first of a trilogy)*

CONTRIBUTIONS:
The Magnificent Cloak in Behind the Hijab, Monsoon Press (2009)

UPCOMING:
Sundari's Footsteps *(the second novel in the trilogy)*

POETRY:

I: A Woman Speaking Up
(An anthology of poems to help raise awareness about emotional domestic abuse) (2020)

CONTRIBUTIONS:
BLAZE (2020) (poems inspired by Bridget Riley as part of the exhibition at The Hayward Gallery)

PHOTOGRAPHY:

Glimpses of Love: Hands in Business
(Wandsworth Arts Festival, London, 2014)

40 Faces of Prayer in Jerusalem
(Iona Community, Iona, Scotland, 2017)

CONTRIBUTIONS:
A day in the life of Putney (London Fringe Arts Festival, 2014)

UPCOMING BOOK: *SUNDARI'S FOOTSTEPS*

Sundari's Footsteps is the second book in a trilogy about Shakti's maternal lineage.

Sundari is Grandma.

Sundari's Footsteps unravels the life of Sundari. From being promised for marriage at six years old and becoming a child bride a few years later, this novel reveals moments, joys and hardships, which she never spoke about until a year before her death at seventy-one years old when Shakti looked after her.

Condemned at thirteen for not having borne a child yet, this beauty turns into a bald and scrawny ghost of a girl. If only, the British rulers had not forbidden the practice of being burnt alive while holding the corpse of her older husband. If only she had jumped on the pyre. There was no such solace for her.

How did harshness mingle with such a fierce sense of duty? How did her cruelty fester next to her devotion to God? Was there ever any love? Rage? Penance? Karma? What is it?

No child of hers will crawl on the floor unable to walk. Her son will stay in school with the white people. No one will trample her on the inside, even if she is just a woman and women should know their place. No!